LCM CLA

An Anthology of Verse

Selected by
Rex Satchwell & Patricia Finch

LCM Publications

First published in 1997
by LCM Publications
Thames Valley University, St Mary's Road, London W5 5RF

Printed in England by The Basingstoke Press Ltd

Selection © LCM Publications 1997

This book is sold subject to the condition that it shall not, by way of trade or otherwise, be lent, re-sold, hired out or otherwise circulated without the publisher's prior consent in any form of binding or cover other than that in which it is published and without a similar condition including this condition being imposed on the subsequent purchaser.

ISBN 0-9528375-1-X

LL122254

Contents

Thomas Wyatt (1503?-1542)
Blame Not My Lute   11
Forget Not Yet   13
The Lover Compareth his State to a Ship   14
in Perilous Storm Tossed on the Sea

Sir Walter Raleigh (1552?-1618)
As You Came From the Holy Land   18
A Description of Love   20
The Passionate Man's Pilgrimage   21

Edmund Spenser (1552?-1599)
Fresh Spring, the herald of love's mighty king   15
Behold, O Man *from* The Faerie Queene   16
There is a meadow *from* Prothalamion   17

Sir Philip Sidney (1554-1586)
Rural Poesy   23
The Nightingale   24
The Bargain   25

John Lyly (1554?-1606)
Syrinx   25
Cupid and Campaspe   26
Daphne   27

Michael Drayton (1563-1631)
Agincourt   28
The Crier   30
Since there's no help, come let us kiss and part   31

William Shakespeare (1564-1616)
Shall I compare thee to a summer's day?   32
When to the sessions of sweet silent thought   33
Fidele   34
When in disgrace with fortune and men's eyes   35

Thomas Campion (1567?-1619)
Never Weather-Beaten Sail   35
Laura   36
Follow Thy Fair Sun   37

Thomas Dekker (1570?-1641?)
A Cradle Song	38
Song	38
Oh, the Month of May	39

John Donne (1573-1631)
The Canonization	40
Song	42
A Hymn to God the Father	43

Thomas Ford (c.1580-1648)
There is a lady sweet and kind	44

John Milton (1608-1674)
Nymphs and Shepherds, Dance No More	45
On His Blindness	46
At A Solemn Music	47

John Dryden (1631-1700)
Phyllis	48
To the Memory of Mr Oldham	49
Happy the Man	50

William Congreve (1670-1729)
False though She Be	51
A Hue and Cry after Fair Amoret	51

Alexander Pope (1688-1744)
On a Certain Lady at Court	52
Know Thyself *from* An Essay on Man	53
from:the Rape of the Lock	54

Oliver Goldsmith (1730-1774)
Song	57
The Deserted Village *from* The Deserted Village	57
The Village Schoolmaster *from* The Deserted Village	58

William Blake (1757-1827)
The Piper	60
O rose, thou art sick!	61
The Garden of Love	61
London	62
Tiger, Tiger burning bright	63

William Wordsworth (1770-1850)
She Was a Phantom of Delight	64
from Ode: Intimations of Immortality from Recollections of Early Childhood	65
Louisa	66

Samuel Taylor Coleridge (1772-1834)
Work without Hope	67
Hunting Song	68
Kubla Khan	68

Jane Taylor (1783-1824)
Twinkle, twinkle, little star	71

Percy Bysshe Shelley (1792-1822)
Ode to the West Wind	72
Love's Philosophy	76
To Jane: The Keen Stars Were Twinkling	77

John Clare (1793-1864)
Little Trotty Wagtail	78
The Vixen	79
Autumn	79

John Keats (1795-1821)
To Autumn	80
On First Looking into Chapman's Homer	82
Song	83

Sara Coleridge (1802-1850)
January Brings the Snow	84
The Mother	85
Trees	86

Elizabeth Barratt Browning (1806-1861)
A Musical Instrument	86
Grief	88
A Man's Requirements	89

Alfred, Lord Tennyson (1809-1892)
The Miller's Daughter	92
Tears, Idle Tears *from* The Princess	93
I come from haunts of coots and hern *from* The Brook	94

Robert Browning (1812-1889)
Pippa's Song	95
My Last Duchess	95
from: The Pied Piper	97

Charles Kingsley (1819-1875)
Three Fishers went Sailing	102
A Farewell	103
The Sands of Dee	103

Matthew Arnold (1822-1888)
Dover Beach   104
Philomela   106
Requiescat   107

Emily Dickinson (1830-1886)
Because I could not stop for Death   108
The Waking Year   109
Like Rain it sounded till it curved   110

Christina Rossetti (1830-1894)
The Wind   111
Song   111
from: Goblin Market   112
Uphill   118
Remember   119

Laurence Alma Tadema (1836-1912)
Little Girls   120

Alice Meynell (1847-1922)
The Rainy Summer   121
In Manchester Square   122
A Thrush Before Dawn   122

Edith Nesbit (1858-1924)
Child's Song in Spring   124
In the Cabinet Drawer   125
Baby's Birthday   126

Rupert Brooke (1887-1915)
The Soldier   127
Clouds   128

Wilfred Owen (1893-1918)
Futility   129
The Send-Off   130
Greater Love   131

Anonymous Poems
The north wind doth blow   132
Curley locks, curley locks   133
The Streets of Laredo   133
Poor but Honest   135
The Riddling Knight   137

Charles Collins & Fred W Leigh
The Bridesmaid   138

 *Introduction*

The London College of Music is very pleased to be publishing this anthology, designed, originally, to accompany the syllabus in Speech, Drama and Communication for the years 1997-2000.

It is, perhaps, particularly appropriate that we celebrate the millennium with a collection of poems which, because of their enduring quality, are entitled to be known as 'classics'. These poems constitute an aspect of the past we can value and enjoy for the whole of our lives.

There are, of course, many ways in which we can enjoy a poem: we may read it quietly and study its form and content and this may well lead us to read other poems by the same author or want to identify the period in which the piece was written and compare it with the work of other poets. Equally, we may speak the poem aloud or listen to someone else doing so, in which case we shall also need to focus our performance skills on the poem and use our supporting knowledge to find the poet's voice in what we speak or hear.

This anthology, therefore, is entirely composed of poems suitable for speaking aloud but the poems are also arranged so that their place in literary history can be quickly identified. In some cases we have included extra poems to those simply required by the syllabus and in others have included extracts which we hope will inspire you to find the entire poem and enjoy it.

L.C.M Classics is a rich and varied collection covering almost every aspect of our human lives. Allow yourself to respond to the humour, joy, sadness, narrative and imagery, and share this pleasure with others in your Examination and Recital work.

Thomas Wyatt (1503?-1542)

Blame Not My Lute

Blame not my lute! for he must sound
Of this or that as liketh me;
For lack of wit the lute is bound
To give such tunes as pleaseth me;
Though my songs be somewhat strange,
And speaks such words as touch thy change,
Blame not my lute!

My lute, alas! doth not offend,
Though that perforce he must agree
To sound such tunes as I intend
To sing to them that heareth me;
Then though my songs be somewhat plain
And toucheth some that use to feign,
Blame not my lute!

My lute and strings may not deny,
But as I strike they must obey;
Break not them then so wrongfully,
But wreak thyself some other way;
And though the songs which I indite
Do quit thy change with rightful spite,
Blame not my lute!

Spite asketh spite, and changing change,
And falsëd faith must needs be known;
The faults so great, the case so strange,
Of right it must abroad be blown;
Then since that by thine own desart
My songs do tell how true thou art,
Blame not my lute!

Blame but thyself that hast misdone,
And well deservëd to have blame;
Change thou thy way, so evil begun,
And then my lute shall sound that same;
But if till then my fingers play
By thy desart their wonted way,
Blame not my lute!

Farewell, unknown! for though thou break
My strings in spite with great disdain,
Yet have I found out, for thy sake,
Strings for to string my lute again:
And if, perchance, this foolish rhyme
Do make thee blush at any time,
Blame not my lute!

Forget Not Yet

Forget not yet the tried intent
Of such a truth as I have meant;
My great travail so gladly spent,
Forget not yet!

Forget not yet when first began
The weary life ye know, since whan
The suit, the service, none tell can;
Forget not yet!

Forget not yet the great assays,
The cruel wrong, the scornful ways,
The painful patience in denays,
Forget not yet!

Forget not yet, forget not this -
How long ago hath been, and is,
The mind that never meant amiss,
Forget not yet!

Forget not then thine own approved,
The which so long hath thee so loved,
Whose steadfast faith yet never moved:
Forget not this!

The Lover Compareth his State to a Ship in Perilous Storm Tossed on the Sea

My gallery, chargëd with forgetfulness,
Thorough sharp seas in winter nights doth pass
'Tween rock and rock; and eke my foe, alas,
That is my lord, steereth with cruelness;
And every hour, a thought in readiness,
As though that death were light in such a case;
An endless wind doth tear the sail apace
Of forcëd sighs, and trusty fearfulness;
A rain of tears, a cloud of dark disdain,
Hath done the wearied cords great hinderance;
Wreathëd with error and eke with ignorance,
The stars be hid that led me to this pain.
Drownëd is reason that should me comfòrt,
And I remain, despairing of the port.

Edmund Spenser (1552?-1599)

Sonnet

Fresh Spring, the herald of love's mighty king,
In whose coat-armour richly are displayed
All sorts of flowers, the which on earth do spring,
In goodly colours gloriously arrayed,
Go to my Love, where she is careless laid
Yet in her winter's bower not well awake;
Tell her the joyous time will not be stayed
Unless she do him by the forelock take.
Bid her, therefore, herself soon ready make,
To wait on Love amongst his lovely crew;
Where every one that misseth then her make,
Shall be by him amerced with penance due.
Make haste therefore, sweet Love, whilst it is prime,
For none can call again the passëd time.

Behold, O Man

Behold, O man, that toilsome pains dost take,
The flowers, the fields, and all that pleasant grows,
How they themselves do thine ensample make,
Whiles nothing-envious nature them forth throws
Out of her fruitful lap; how, no man knows,
They spring, they bud, they blossom fresh and fair,
And deck the world with their rich pompous shows;
Yet no man for them taketh pains or care,
Yet no man to them can his careful pains compare.

The lily, lady of the flowering field,
The flower-de-luce, her lovely paramour,
Bid thee to them thy fruitless labours yield,
And soon leave off this toilsome weary stour:
Lo! lo, how brave she decks her bounteous bower,
With silken curtains and gold coverlets,
Therein to shroud her sumptuous belamour,
Yet neither spins nor cards ne cares nor frets,
But to her mother nature all her care she lets.

Why then dost thou, O man, that of them all
Art lord, and eke of nature sovereign,
Wilfully make thyself a wretched thrall,
And waste thy joyous hours in needless pain,
Seeking for danger and adventures vain?
What boot it all to have, and nothing use?
Who shall him rue, that, swimming in the main,
Will die for thirst, and water doth refuse?
Refuse such fruitless toil, and present pleasures choose.

The verses above are from "The Fairie Queene", a very long poem. The following lines are from "Prothalamion", a quite long poem. You may like to look them up.

> There in a meadow by the river's side
> A flock of nymphs I chancëd to espy,
> All lovely daughters of the flood thereby,
> With goodly greenish locks all loose untied
> As each had been a bride;
> And each one had a little wicker basket
> Made of fine twigs entrailëd curiously,
> In which they gathered flowers to fill their flasket,
> And with fine fingers cropped full featiously
> The tender stalks on high.
> Of every sort which in that meadow grew
> They gathered some; the violet, pallid blue,
> The little daisy that at evening closes,
> The virgin lily and the primrose true,
> With store of vermeil roses,
> To deck their bridegrooms' posies
> Against the bridal day, which was not long:
> Sweet Thames! run softly, till I end my song.

Sir Walter Raleigh (1552?-1618)

As You Came From the Holy Land

As you came from the holy land
Of Walsingham,
Met you not with my true Love
By the way as you came?

'How shall I know your true Love,
That have met many one,
As I went to the holy land,
That have come, that have gone?'

She is neither white, nor brown,
But as the heavens fair;
There is none hath a form so divine
In the earth, or the air.

'Such a one did I meet, good sir!
Such an angelic face,
Who like a queen, like a nymph, did appear
By her gait, by her grace.'

She hath left me here all alone,
All alone, as unknown,
Who sometimes did me lead with herself,
And me loved as her own.

'What's the cause that she leaves you alone,
And a new way doth take,
Who loved you once as her own,
And her joy did you make?'

I have loved her all my youth;
But now old, as you see,
Love likes not the falling fruit
From the withered tree.

Know that Love is a careless child,
And forgets promise past;
He is blind, he is deaf when he list,
And in faith never fast.

His desire is a dureless content,
And a trustless joy:
He is won with a world of despair,
And is lost with a toy.

Of womenkind such indeed is the love,
Or the word love abused,
Under which many childish desires
And conceits are excused.

But true love is a durable fire,
In the mind ever burning,
Never sick, never old, never dead,
From itself never turning.

A Description of Love

Now what is love, I pray thee tell?
It is that fountain and that well
Where pleasure and repentance dwell.
It is perhaps that sauncing bell
That tolls all into heaven or hell:
And this is love, as I hear tell.

Yet what is love, I pray thee say?
It is a work on holy day.
It is December matched with May,
When lusty bloods in fresh array
Hear ten months after of the play:
And this is love, as I hear say.

Yet what is love, I pray thee sain?
It is a sunshine mixed with rain.
It is a tooth-ache, or like pain;
It is a game where none doth gain;
The lass saith No, and would full fain:
And this is love, as I hear sain.

Yet what is love, I pray thee say?
It is a yea, it is a nay,
A pretty kind of sporting fray;
It is a thing will soon away;
Then take the vantage while you may:
And this is love, as I hear say.

Yet what is love, I pray thee show?
A thing that creeps, it cannot go;
A prize that passeth to and fro;
A thing for one, a thing for mo;
And he that proves must find it so:
And this is love, sweet friend, I trow.

The Passionate Man's Pilgrimage

Give me my scallop-shell of Quiet;
My staff of Faith to walk upon;
My scrip of Joy, immortal diet;
My bottle of Salvatïon;
My gown of Glory, hope's true gage;
And thus I'll take my pilgrimage.
Blood must be my body's balmer -
No other balm will there be given -
Whilst my soul, like a white palmer,
Travels to the land of Heaven;
Over the silver mountains,
Where spring the nectar fountains -
And there I'll kiss
The bowl of Bliss,
And drink my eternal fill
On every milken hill:
My soul will be a-dry before,
But after it will ne'er thirst more.
And by the happy blissful way,
More peaceful pilgrims I shall see,

That have shook off their gowns of clay,
And go apparelled fresh like me:
I'll bring them first
To slake their thirst,
And then to taste those nectar suckets,
At the clear wells
Where sweetness dwells,
Drawn up by saints in crystal buckets.
And when our bottles and all we
Are filled with immortality,
Then the holy paths we'll travel,
Strewed with rubies thick as gravel.
Ceilings of diamonds, sapphire floors,
High walls of coral, and pearl bowers.
From thence to Heaven's bribeless hall,
Where no corrupted voices brawl;
No conscience molten into gold;
Nor forged accusers bought and sold;
No cause deferred; nor vain-spent journey;
For there Christ is the King's Attorney,
Who pleads for all without degrees,
And he hath angels, but no fees.
When the grand twelve million jury
Of our sins and sinful fury,
'Gainst our souls black verdicts give,
Christ pleads his death, and then we live.
Be thou my speaker, taintless Pleader,
Unblotted Lawyer, true Proceeder!
Thou movest salvation even for alms,
Not with a bribëd lawyer's palms.
And this is my eternal plea
To him that made heaven, earth, and sea,

Seeing my flesh must die so soon,
And want a head to dine next noon, -
Just at the stroke, when my veins start and spread,
Set on my soul and everlasting head:
Then am I ready, like a palmer fit,
To tread those blest paths which before I writ.

Sir Philip Sidney (1554-1586)

Rural Poesy

O words, which fall like summer dew on me!
O breath, more sweet than is the growing bean!
O tongue, in which all honeyed liquors be!
O voice, that doth the thrush in shrillness stain! -
Do you say still this is her promise due,
That she is mine, as I to her am true.

Gay hair, more gay than straw when harvest lies!
Lips, red and plump as cherry's ruddy side!
Eyes fair and great, like fair great ox's eyes!
O breast, in which two white sheep swell in pride! -
Join you with me to seal this promise due,
That she be mine, as I to her am true.

But thou white skin, as white as curds well pressed,
So smooth as, sleek-stone like, it smooths each part!
And thou dear flesh, as soft as wool new dressed,
And yet as hard as brawn made hard by art! -
First four but say, next four their saying seal;
But you must pay the gage of promised weal.

The Nightingale

The nightingale, as soon as April bringeth
Unto her rested sense a perfect waking,
While late bare earth, proud of new clothing, springeth,
Sings out her woes, a thorn her song-book making;
And, mournfully bewailing,
Her throat in tunes expresseth
What grief her breast oppresseth,
For Tereus' force on her chaste will prevailing.

O Philomela fair! oh, take some gladness
That here is juster cause of plaintful sadness:
Thine earth now springs, mine fadeth;
Thy thorn without, my thorn my heart invadeth.

Alas! she hath no other cause of anguish
But Tereus' love, on her by strong hand wroken;
Wherein she suffering, all her spirits languish,
Full womanlike complains her will was broken.
But I, who, daily craving,
Can not have to content me,
Have more cause to lament me,
Since wanting is more woe than too much having.

O Philomela fair! oh, take some gladness
That here is juster cause of plaintful sadness:
Thine earth now springs, mine fadeth;
Thy thorn without, my thorn my heart invadeth.

The Bargain

My true Love hath my heart, and I have his,
By just exchange one for the other given:
I hold his dear, and mine he cannot miss;
There never was a better bargain driven.
His heart in me keeps me and him in one,
My heart in him his thoughts and senses guides:
He loves my heart, for once it was his own;
I cherish his because in me it bides.
His heart his wound receivëd from my sight,
My heart was wounded with his wounded heart;
For as from me, on him his hurt did light,
So still methought in me his hurt did smart.
Both, equal hurt, in this change sought our bliss:
My true Love hath my heart, and I have his.

John Lyly (1554?-1606)

Syrinx

Pan's Syrinx was a girl indeed,
Though now she's turned into a reed;
From that dear reed Pan's pipe does come,
A pipe that strikes Apollo dumb;
Nor flute, nor lute, nor gittern can
So chant it as the pipe of Pan:
Cross-gartered swains and dairy girls,
With faces smug and round as pearls,
When Pan's shrill pipe begins to play,
With dancing wear out night and day:

The bagpipe's drone his hum lays by
When Pan sounds up his minstrelsy;
His minstrelsy! oh, base! this quill -
Which at my mouth with wind I fill -
Puts me in mind, though her I miss,
That still my Syrinx' lips I kiss.

Cupid and Campaspe

Cupid and my Campaspe played
At cards for kisses - Cupid paid:
He stakes his quiver, bow and arrows,
His mother's doves, and team of sparrows;
Loses them too; then down he throws
The coral of his lip, the rose
Growing on 's cheek (but none knows how);
With these, the crystal of his brow,
And then the dimple of his chin
All these did my Campaspe win.
At last he set her both his eyes,
She won, and Cupid blind did rise.
O Love! has she done this to thee?
What shall, alas, become of me?

Daphne

My Daphne's hair is twisted gold.
Bright stars a-piece her eyes do hold,
My Daphne's brow enthrones the graces,
My Daphne's beauty stains all faces;
On Daphne's cheek grow rose and cherry,
On Daphne's lip a sweeter berry;
Daphne's snowy hand but touched does melt,
And then no heavenlier warmth is felt;
My Daphne's voice tunes all the spheres,
My Daphne's music charms all ears.
Fond am I thus to sing her praise;
These glories now are turned to bays.

Michael Drayton (1563-1631)

AGINCOURT

I
Fair stood the wind for France
When we our sails advance,
Nor now to prove our chance
　Longer will tarry;
But putting to the main,
At Caux, the mouth of Seine,
With all his martial train
　Landed King Harry.

II
And taking many a fort,
Furnished in warlike sort,
Marcheth towards Agincourt
　In happy hour;
Skirmishing day by day
With those that stopped his way,
Where the French general lay
　With all his power;

III
Which, in his height of pride,
King Henry to deride,
His ransom to provide
　To the king sending;
Which he neglects the while
As from a nation vile,
Yet with an angry smile
　Their fall portending.

IV
And turning to his men,
Quoth our brave Henry then,
'Though they to one be ten,
　Be not amazèd;
Yet have we well begun,
Battles so bravely won
Have ever to the sun
　By fame been raisèd.

V
'And for myself,' quoth he,
'This my full rest shall be:
England ne'er mourn for me,
　Nor more esteem me;
Victor I will remain
Or on this earth lie slain,
Never shall she sustain
　Loss to redeem me.

VI
'Poitiers and Cressy tell,
When most their pride did swell,
Under our swords they fell;
　No less our skill is
Than when our grandsire great,
Claiming the regal seat,
By many a warlike feat
　Lopped the French lilies.'

VII
The Duke of York so dread
The eager vaward led;
With the main Henry sped,
　Amongst his henchmen.
Exeter had the rear,
A braver man not there;
O Lord, how hot they were
　On the false Frenchmen!

VIII
They now to fight are gone,
Armour on armour shone,
Drum now to drum did groan,
　To hear was wonder:
That with the cries they make
The very earth did shake;
Trumpet to trumpet spake,
　Thunder to thunder.

IX

Well it thine age became,
O noble Erpingham,
Which didst the signal aim
   To our hid forces!
When, from a meadow by,
Like a storm suddenly
The English archer
   Struck the French horses:

X

With Spanish yew so strong,
Arrows a cloth-yard long,
That like to serpents stung,
   Piercing the weather;
None from his fellow starts,
But, playing manly parts,
And like true English hearts,
   Stuck close together.

XI

When down their bows they threw
And forth their bilbos drew,
And on the French they flew,
   Not one was tardy;
Arms were from shoulders sent,
Scalps to the teeth were rent,
Down the French peasants went:
   Our men were hardy.

XII

This while our noble King,
His broad sword brandishing,
Down the French host did ding
   As to o'erwhelm it;
And many a deep wound lent,
His arms with blood besprent,
And many a cruel dent
   Bruisëd his helmet.

XIII

Gloucester, that duke so good,
Next of the royal blood,
For famous England stood
   With his brave brother:
Clarence, in steel so bright,
Though but a maiden knight,
Yet in that furious fight
   Scarce such another.

XIV

Warwick in blood did wade,
Oxford the foe invade,
And cruel slaughter made
   Still as they ran up;
Suffolk his axe did ply,
Beaumont and Willoughby
Bare them right doughtily,
   Ferrers and Fanhope.

XV

Upon Saint Crispin's day
Fought was this noble fray,
Which fame did not delay
   To England to carry;
Oh, when shall English men
With such acts fill a pen?
Or England breed again
   Such a King Harry?

The Crier

Good folk, for gold or hire,
But help me to a Crier!
For my poor Heart is run astray
After two Eyes, that passed this way.
O yes! O yes! O yes!
If there be any man,
In town or country, can
Bring my Heart again,
I'll please him for his pain.
And by these marks, I will you show
That only I this Heart do owe:
It is a wounded Heart,
Wherein yet sticks the dart;
Every piece sore hurt throughout it,
Faith and troth writ round about it;
It was a tame Heart, and a dear,
And never used to roam:
But having got this haunt, I fear
'Twill hardly stay at home.
For God's sake, walking by the way
If you my Heart do see,
Either impound it for a stray,
Or send it back to me!

Sonnet

Since there's no help, come let us kiss and part -
Nay, I have done: you get no more of me;
And I am glad, yea, glad with all my heart,
That thus so cleanly I myself can free.
Shake hands for ever, cancel all our vows,
And when we meet at any time again,
Be it not seen in either of our brows
That we one jot of former love retain.
Now at the last gasp of love's latest breath,
When, his pulse failing, Passion speechless lies,
When Faith is kneeling by his bed of death,
And Innocence is closing up his eyes, -
Now, if though wouldst, when all have given him over,
From death to life thou might'st him yet recover!

William Shakespeare (1564-1616)

Sonnet

Shall I compare thee to a summer's day?
Thou art more lovely and more temperate:
Rough winds do shake the darling buds of May,
And summer's lease hath all too short a date:
Sometime too hot the eye of heaven shines,
And often is his gold complexion dimmed:
And every fair from fair sometime declines,
By chance, or nature's changing course, untrimmed.
But thy eternal summer shall not fade,
Nor lose possession of that fair thou ow'st,
Nor shall death brag thou wander'st in his shade,
When in eternal lines to time thou grow'st;
So long as men can breathe, or eyes can see,
So long lives this, and this gives life to thee.

Sonnet

When to the sessions of sweet silent thought
I summon up remembrance of things past,
I sigh the lack of many a thing I sought,
And with old woes new wail my dear time's waste;
Then can I drown an eye, unused to flow,
For precious friends hid in death's dateless night,
And weep afresh love's long since cancelled woe,
And moan the expense of many a vanished sight.
Then can I grieve at grievances foregone,
And heavily from woe to woe tell o'er
The sad account of fore-bemoanëd moan,
Which I new pay as if not paid before:
But if the while I think on thee, dear friend,
All losses are restored, and sorrows end.

Fidele

Fear no more the heat o' the sun,
Nor the furious winter's rages;
Thou thy worldly task hast done,
Home art gone, and ta'en thy wages:
Golden lads and girls all must,
As chimney-sweepers, come to dust.

Fear no more the frown o' the great;
Thou art past the tyrant's stroke:
Care no more to clothe and eat;
To thee the reed is as the oak:
The sceptre, learning, physic, must
All follow this, and come to dust.

Fear no more the lightning-flash,
Nor the all-dreaded thunder-stone;
Fear not slander, censure rash;
Thou hast finished joy and moan:
All lovers young, all lovers must
Consign to thee, and come to dust.

No exorciser harm thee!
Nor no witchcraft charm thee!
Ghost unlaid forbear thee!
Nothing ill come near thee!
Quiet consummation have;
And renownëd be thy grave!

Sonnet

When, in disgrace with fortune and men's eyes,
I all alone beweep my outcast state,
And trouble deaf heaven with my bootless cries,
And look upon myself, and curse my fate,
Wishing me like to one more rich in hope,
Featured like him, like him with friends possessed,
Desiring this man's art and that man's scope,
With what I most enjoy contented least;
Yet in these thoughts myself almost despising,
Haply I think on thee: and then my state,
Like to the lark at break of day arising
From sullen earth, sings hymns at heaven's gate;
For thy sweet love remembered such wealth brings
That then I scorn to change my state with Kings.

Thomas Campion (1567?-1619)

Never Weather-Beaten Sail

Never weather-beaten sail more willing bent to shore,
Never tired pilgrim's limbs affected slumber more,
Than my weary sprite now longs to fly out of my troubled breast.
Oh, come quickly, sweetest Lord, and take my soul to rest!

Ever blooming are the joys of heaven's high paradise,
Cold age deafs not there our ears nor vapour dims our eyes:
Glory there the sun outshines, whose beams the blessëd only see.
Oh, come quickly, glorious Lord, and raise my sprite to thee!

Laura

Rose-cheeked Laura, come;
Sing thou smoothly with thy beauty's
Silent music, either other
Sweetly gracing.

Lovely forms do flow
From concent divinely framëd;
Heaven is music, and thy beauty's
Birth is heavenly.

These dull notes we sing
Discords need for helps to grace them;
Only beauty purely loving
Knows no discord;

But still moves delight,
Like clear springs renewed by flowing,
Ever perfect, ever in them-
Selves eternal.

Follow Thy Fair Sun

Follow thy fair sun, unhappy shadow!
Though thou be black as night,
And she made all of light,
Yet follow thy fair sun, unhappy shadow!

Follow her, whose light thy light depriveth!
Though here thou liv'st disgraced,
And she in heaven is placed,
Yet follow her whose light the world reviveth!

Follow those pure beams, whose beauty burneth!
That so have scorchëd thee
As thou still black must be
Till her kind beams thy black to brightness turneth.

Follow her, while yet her glory shineth!
There comes a luckless night
That will dim all her light;
And this the black unhappy shade divineth.

Follow still, since so thy fates ordainëd!
The sun must have his shade,
Till both at once do fade,
The sun still proud, the shadow still disdainëd.

Thomas Dekker (1570?-1641?)

A Cradle Song

Golden slumbers kiss your eyes,
Smiles awake you when you rise.
Sleep, pretty wantons, do not cry,
And I will sing a lullaby:
Rock them, rock them, lullaby.

Care is heavy, therefore sleep you;
You are care, and care must keep you.
Sleep, pretty wantons, do not cry,
And I will sing a lullaby:
Rock them, rock them, lullaby.

Song

Virtue's branches wither, virtue pines,
O pity, pity, and alack the time!
Vice doth flourish, vice in glory shines,
Her gilded boughs above the cedar climb.

Vice hath golden cheeks, O pity, pity!
She in every land doth monarchize:
Virtue is exiled from every city,
Virtue is a fool, vice only wise.

O pity, pity! virtue weeping dies,
Vice laughs to see her faint, alack the time!
This sinks; with painted wings the other flies:
Alack, that best should fall, and bad should climb!

O pity, pity, pity! mourn, not sing!
Vice is a saint, virtue an underling.
Vice doth flourish, vice in glory shines,
Virtue's branches wither, virtue pines.

Oh, the Month of May!

Oh, the month of May, the merry month of May,
So frolic, so gay, and so green, so green, so green!
Oh, and then did I unto my true Love say,
Sweet Peg, thou shalt be my Summer's Queen.

Now the nightingale, the pretty nightingale,
The sweetest singer in all the forest's quire,
Entreats thee, sweet Peggy, to hear thy true Love's tale:
Lo, yonder she sitteth, her breast against a brier.

But oh, I spy the cuckoo, the cuckoo, the cuckoo;
See where she sitteth; come away, my joy:
Come away, I prithee, I do not like the cuckoo
Should sing where my Peggy and I kiss and toy.

Oh, the month of May, the merry month of May,
So frolic, so gay, and so green, so green, so green;
And then did I unto my true Love say,
Sweet Peg, thou shalt be my Summer's Queen.

John Donne (1573-1631)

The Canonization

For God's sake hold your tongue, and let me love;
Or chide my palsy, or my gout;
My five grey hairs, or ruined fortune flout;
With wealth your state, your mind with arts improve;
Take you a course, get you a place,
Observe his Honour, or his Grace;
Or the King's real, or his stampëd face
Contemplate; what you will, approve,
So you will let me love.

Alas! alas! who's injured by my love?
What merchant's ships have my sighs drowned?
Who says my tears have overflowed his ground?
When did my colds a forward spring remove?
When did the heats which my veins fill
Add one more to the plaguy bill?
Soldiers find wars, and lawyers find out still
Litigious men, which quarrels move,
Though she and I do love.

Call us what you will, we are made such by love;
Call her one, me another fly,
We are tapers too, and at our own cost die,
And we in us find the eagle and the dove.
The phoenix riddle hath more wit
By us; we two being one, are it;
So, to one neutral thing both sexes fit,
We die and rise the same, and prove
Mysterious by this love.

We can die by it, if not live by love,
And if unfit for tombs and hearse
Our legends be, it will be fit for verse;
And if no piece of chronicle we prove,
We'll build in sonnets pretty rooms;
As well a well-wrought urn becomes
The greatest ashes, as half-acre tombs,
And by these hymns all shall approve
Us canonized for love;

And thus invoke us, 'You, whom reverend love
Made one another's hermitage;
You, to whom love was peace, that now is rage;
Who did the whole world's soul contract, and drove
Into the glasses of your eyes,
So made such mirrors, and such spies,
That they did all to you epitomize -
Countries, towns, courts beg from above
A pattern of your love.'

Song

Go and catch a falling star;
Get with child a mandrake root;
Tell me where all past years are,
Or who cleft the Devil's foot;
Teach me to hear mermaids singing,
Or to keep off envy's stinging.
And find
What wind
Serves to advance an honest mind.

If thou be'st born to strange sights,
Things invisible to see,
Ride ten thousand days and nights
Till age snow white hairs on thee;
Thou, when thou return'st, wilt tell me
All strange wonders that befell thee,
And swear
No where
Lives a woman true and fair.

If thou find'st one, let me know;
Such a pilgrimage were sweet.
Yet do not; I would not go,
Though at next door we might meet.
Though she were true when you met her,
And last till you write your letter,
Yet she
Will be
False, ere I come, to two or three.

A Hymn to God the Father

Wilt thou forgive that sin where I begun,
Which was my sin, though it were done before?
Wilt though forgive that sin, through which I run,
And do run still, though still I do deplore?
When thou hast done, thou hast not done,
For I have more.

Wilt thou forgive that sin which I have won
Others to sin, and made my sin their door?
Wilt thou forgive that sin which I did shun
A year or two, but wallowed in, a score?
When thou hast done, thou hast not done,
For I have more.

I have a sin of fear, that when I have spun
My last thread, I shall perish on the shore;
But swear by thyself, that at my death thy Son
Shall shine, as he shines now and heretofore:
And, having done that, thou hast done,
I fear no more.

Thomas Ford (c.1580-1648)

There is a Lady sweet and kind
***from:** Music of Sundry Kinds (1607)*

There is a Lady sweet and kind,
Was never face so pleased my mind;
I did but see her passing by,
And yet I love her till I die.

Her gesture, motion, and her smiles,
Her wit, her voice my heart beguiles,
Beguiles my heart, I know not why,
And yet I love her till I die.

Cupid is wingèd and doth range,
Her country so my love doth change:
But change she earth, or change she sky,
Yet will I love her till I die.

John Milton (1608-1674)

Nymphs and Shepherds, Dance No More

Nymphs and shepherds, dance no more
By sandy Ladon's lilied banks;
On old Lycaeus or Cyllene hoar,
Trip no more in twilight ranks;
Though Erymanth your loss deplore,
A better soil shall give ye thanks.
From the stony Maenalus
Bring your flocks and live with us;
Here ye shall have greater grace,
To serve the Lady of this place.
Though Syrinx your Pan's mistress were,
Yet Syrinx well might wait on her.
Such a rural queen
All Arcadia hath not seen.

On His Blindness

When I consider how my light is spent
Ere half my days, in this dark world and wide,
And that one talent which is death to hide
Lodged with me useless, though my soul more bent
To serve therewith my Maker, and present
My true account, lest he returning chide;
Doth God exact day-labour, light denied?
I fondly ask; but Patience, to prevent
That murmur, soon replies, God doth not need
Either man's work, or his own gifts: who best
Bear his mild yoke, they serve him best: his state
Is kingly; thousands at his bidding speed
And post o'er land and ocean without rest:
They also serve who only stand and wait.

At a Solemn Music

Blest pair of sirens, pledges of Heaven's joy,
Sphere-born harmonious sisters, Voice and Verse,
Wed your divine sounds, and mixed power employ,
Dead things with inbreathed sense able to pierce;
And to our high-raised phantasy present
That undisturbëd song of pure concent
Aye sung before the sapphire-coloured throne
To him that sits thereon,
With saintly shout and solemn jubilee;
Where the bright seraphim in burning row
Their loud uplifted angel-trumpets blow;
And the cherubic host in thousand quires
Touch their immortal harps of golden wires,
With those just spirits that wear victorious palms,
Hymns devout and holy psalms
Singing everlastingly:
That we on earth, with undiscording voice,
May rightly answer that melodious noise;
As once we did, till disproportioned sin
Jarred against nature's chime, and with harsh din
Broke the fair music that all creatures made
To their great Lord, whose love their motion swayed
In perfect diapason, whilst they stood
In first obedience, and their state of good.
O may we soon again renew that song,
And keep in tune with Heaven, till God ere long
To his celestial consort us unite,
To live with him, and sing in endless morn of light!

John Dryden (1631-1700)

Phyllis

Wherever I am, and whatever I do,
My Phyllis is still in my mind:
When angry I mean not to Phyllis to go,
My feet of themselves the way find:
Unknown to myself I am just at her door,
And when I would rail I can bring out no more
Than, 'Phyllis, too fair and unkind!'

When Phyllis I see, my heart bounds in my breast,
And the love I would stifle is shown:
But, asleep or awake, I am never at rest
When from my eyes Phyllis is gone!
Sometimes a sad dream does delude my sad mind:
But, alas, when I wake and no Phyllis I find,
How I sigh to myself all alone!

Should a king be my rival in her I adore,
He should offer his treasure in vain :
O let me alone to be happy and poor,
And give me my Phyllis again:
Let Phyllis be mine, and but ever be kind,
I could to a desert with her be confined,
And envy no monarch his reign.

Alas, I discover too much of my love,
And she too well knows her own power!
She makes me each day a new martyrdom prove,
And makes me grow jealous of each hour.
But let her each minute torment my poor mind,
I had rather love Phyllis both false and unkind,
Than ever be freed from her power.

To the Memory of Mr Oldham

Farewell, too little and too lately known,
Whom I began to think and call my own;
For sure our souls were near allied, and thine
Cast in the same poetic mould with mine.
One common note on either lyre did strike,
And knaves and fools we both abhorred alike:
To the same goal did both our studies drive,
The last set out the soonest did arrive,
Thus Nisus fell upon the slippery place,
While his young friend performed and won the race.
O early ripe! to thy abundant store
What could advancing age have added more?
It might (what Nature never gives the young)
Have taught the numbers of thy native tongue.
But Satire needs not those, and Wit will shine
Through the harsh cadence of a rugged line.
A noble error, and but seldom made,
When poets are by too much force betrayed.
Thy generous fruits, though gathered ere their prime
Still showed a quickness; and maturing time

But mellows what we write to the dull sweets of Rhyme.
Once more, hail and farewell; farewell, thou young,
But ah too short, Marcellus of our tongue;
Thy brows with ivy, and with laurels bound;
But Fate and gloomy Night encompass thee around.

Happy the Man

Happy the man, and happy he alone,
He who can call today his own:
He who, secure within, can say,
Tomorrow do thy worst, for I have lived today.
Be fair or foul or rain or shine
The joys I have possessed, in spite of fate, are mine.
Not Heaven itself upon the past has power,
But what has been, has been, and I have had my hour.

This short poem is a translation from the Roman poet, HORACE.

William Congreve (1670-1729)

False though She be

False though she be to me and love,
I'll ne'er pursue revenge;
For still the charmer I approve,
Though I deplore her change.

In hours of bliss we oft have met:
They could not always last;
And though the present I regret,
I'm grateful for the past.

A Hue and Cry after Fair Amoret

Fair Amoret is gone astray -
Pursue and seek her, ev'ry lover;
I'll tell the signs by which you may
The wand'ring Shepherdess discover.

Coquette and coy at once her air,
Both studied, tho' both seem neglected;
Careless she is, with artful care,
Affecting to seem unaffected.

With skill her eyes dart ev'ry glance,
Yet change so soon you'd ne'er suspect them,
For she'd persuade they wound by chance,
Tho' certain aim and art direct them.

She likes herself, yet others hates
For that which in herself she prizes;
And, while she laughs at them, forgets
She is the thing that she despises.

Alexander Pope (1688-1744)

On a Certain Lady at Court

I know the thing that's most uncommon
(Envy, be silent, and attend!)
I know a reasonable woman,
Handsome and witty, yet a friend.

Not warped by passion, awed by rumour,
Not grave through pride, or gay through folly,
An equal mixture of good humour,
And sensible soft melancholy.

'Has she no faults then' (Envy says) 'Sir?'
Yes, she has one, I must aver;
When all the world conspires to praise her,
The woman's deaf, and does not hear.

Know Thyself
from: An Essay on Man

Know then thyself, presume not God to scan;
The proper study of mankind is Man.
Placed on this isthmus of a middle state,
A being darkly wise and rudely great:
With too much knowledge for the Sceptic side,
With too much weakness for the Stoic's pride,
He hangs between; in doubt to act or rest,
In doubt to deem himself a God or Beast,
In doubt his mind or body to prefer;
Born but to die, and reasoning but to err;
Alike in ignorance, his reason such
Whether he thinks too little or too much:
Chaos of thought and passion, all confused;
Still by himself abused, or disabused;
Created half to rise and half to fall;
Great lord of all things, yet a prey to all;
Sole judge of truth, in endless error hurled:
The glory, jest, and riddle of the world!

Pope wrote mainly long poems, "Know Thyself" is from "An Essay on Man". Similarly, "The Rape of the Lock" is too long to print in full. Here are some extracts, but you may still choose your own selections from the poem.

The Rape of the lock

1. from Canto 1

And now, unveil'd, the Toilet stands display'd,
Each silver Vase in mystic order laid.
First, rob'd in white, the Nymph intent adores,
With head uncover'd, the Cosmetic pow'rs.
A heav'nly Image in the glass appears,
To that she bends, to that her eyes she rears;
Th' inferior Priestess, at her altar's side,
Trembling begins the sacred rites of Pride.
Unnumber'd treasures ope at once, and here
The various off'rings of the world appear;
From each she nicely culls with curious toil,
And decks the Goddess with the glitt'ring spoil.
This casket India's glowing gems unlocks,
And all Arabia breathes from yonder box.
The Tortoise here and Elephant unite,
Transform'd to combs, the speckled, and the white.
Here files of pins extend their shining rows,
Puffs, Powders, Patches, Bibles, Billet-doux.
Now awful Beauty puts on all its arms;
The fair each moment rises in her charms,
Repairs her smiles, awakens ev'ry grace,
And calls forth all the wonders of her face;
Sees by degrees a purer blush arise,
And keener lightnings quicken in her eyes.
The busy Sylphs surround their darling care,
These set the head, and those divide the hair,
Some fold the sleeve, whilst others plait the gown;
And Betty's prais'd for labours not her own

2. from Canto 3

Close by those meads, for ever crown'd with flow'rs,
Where Thames with pride surveys his rising tow'rs,
There stands a structure of majestic frame,
Which from the neighb'ring Hampton takes its name,
Here Britain's statesmen oft the fall foredoom
Of foreign Tyrants, and of Nymphs at home;
Here thou, great ANNA! whom three realms obey,
Dost sometimes counsel take - and sometimes Tea.
Hither the Heroes and the Nymphs resort,
To taste awhile the pleasures of a Court;
In various talk th' instructive hours they past,
Who gave the ball, or paid the visit last;
One speaks the glory of the British Queen,
And one describes a charming Indian screen;
A third interprets motions, looks, and eyes;
At ev'ry word a reputation dies.
Snuff, or the fan, supply each pause of chat,
With singing, laughing, ogling, *and all that.*
Mean while, declining from the noon of day,
The sun obliquely shoots his burning ray;
The hungry Judges soon the sentence sign,
And wretches hang that Jury-men may dine;
The merchant from th' Exchange returns in peace,
And the long labours of the Toilet cease.
Belinda now, whom thirst of fame invites,
Burns to encounter two advent'rous Knights,
At Ombre singly to decide their doom;
And swells her breast with conquests yet to come.

3. from Canto 4

On her heav'd bosom hung her drooping head,
Which, with a sigh she rais'd; and thus she said.
'For ever curs'd be this detested day,
Which snatch'd my best, my fav'rite curl away!
Happy! ah ten times happy had I been,
If Hampton-Court these eyes had never seen!
Yet am not I the first mistaken maid,
By love of Courts to num'rous ills betray'd.
Oh had I rather un-admir'd remain'd
In some lone isle, or distant Northern land;
Where the gilt Chariot never marks the way,
Where none learn Ombre, none e'er taste Bohea!
There kept my charms conceal'd from mortal eye,
Like roses, that in deserts bloom and die.
What mov'd my mind with youthful Lords to roam?
O had I stay'd, and said my pray'rs at home!
'Twas this, the morning omens seem'd to tell:
Thrice from my trembling hand the patch-box fell;
The tott'ring China shook without a wind,
Nay Poll sat mute, and Shock was most unkind!
A Sylph too warn'd me of the threats of fate,
In mystic visions, now believ'd too late!
See the poor remnants of these slighted hairs!
My hands shall rend what ev'n thy rapine spares:
These in two sable ringlets taught to break,
Once gave new beauties to the snowy neck;
The sister-lock now sits uncouth, alone,
And in its fellow's fate foresees its own;
Uncurl'd it hangs, the fatal sheers demands,
And tempts, once more, thy sacrilegious hands.
Oh hadst thou, cruel! been content to seize
Hairs less in sight, or any hairs but these!'

Oliver Goldsmith (1730-1774)

Song

When lovely woman stoops to folly,
And finds too late that men betray,
What charm can sooth her melancholy,
What art can wash her guilt away?

The only art her guilt to cover,
To hide her shame from every eye,
To give repentance to her lover,
And wring his bosom - is to die.

Goldsmith did not write many short poems, so here are two well known excerpts from "The Deserted Village". If you enjoy them, why not find the whole poem?

The Deserted Village

Sweet was the sound, when oft at evening's close
Up yonder hill the village murmur rose;
There, as I pass'd with careless steps and slow,
The mingling notes came soften'd from below;
The swain responsive as the milkmaid sung,
The sober herd that low'd to meet their young;
The noisy geese that gabbled o'er the pool,
The playful children just let loose from school,

The watch-dog's voice that bayed the whispering wind,
And the loud laugh that spoke the vacant mind;
These all in sweet confusion sought the shade,
And fill'd each pause the nightingale had made.
But now the sounds of population fail,
No cheerful murmurs fluctuate in the gale,
No busy steps the grass-grown footway tread,
But all the blooming flush of life is fled;
All but yon widow'd, solitary thing,
That feebly bends beside the plashy spring;
She, wretched matron, forced, in age, for bread,
To strip the brook with mantling cresses spread,
To pick her wintry faggot from the thorn,
To seek her nightly shed, and weep till morn;
She only left of all the harmless train,
The sad historian of the pensive plain.

The Village Schoolmaster

Beside yon straggling fence that skirts the way
With blossom'd furze, unprofitably gay,
There, in his noisy mansion, skill'd to rule,
The village master taught his little school:
A man severe he was, and stern to view,
I knew him well, and every truant knew;
Well had the boding tremblers learn'd to trace
The day's disasters in his morning face;
Full well they laugh'd with counterfeited glee
At all his jokes for many a joke had he;

Full well the busy whisper, circling round,
Convey'd the dismal tidings when he frown'd;
Yet he was kind, or if severe in aught,
The love he bore to learning was in fault;
The village all declared how much he knew,
'Twas certain he could write and cipher too;
Lands he could measure, terms and tides presage,
And e'en the story ran that he could gauge:
In arguing too, the parson own'd his skill,
For e'en though vanquish'd, he could argue still;
While words of learned length and thundering sound
Amazed the gazing rustics ranged around;
And still they gazed, and still the wonder grew
That one small head could carry all he knew.

William Blake (1757-1827)

The Piper

Piping down the valleys wild,
Piping songs of pleasant glee,
On a cloud I saw a child,
And he laughing said to me:

'Pipe a song about a Lamb!'
So I piped with merry cheer.
'Piper, pipe that song again;'
So I piped: he wept to hear.

'Drop thy pipe, thy happy pipe;
Sing thy songs of happy cheer.'
So I sung the same again,
While he wept with joy to hear.

'Piper, sit thee down and write
In a book that all may read.'
So he vanished from my sight,
And I plucked a hollow reed.

And I made a rural pen,
And I stained the water clear,
And I wrote my happy songs
Every child may joy to hear.

O rose, thou art sick!

O rose, thou art sick!
The invisible worm
That flies in the night,
In the howling storm,
Has found out thy bed
Of crimson joy,
And his dark secret love
Does thy life destroy.

The Garden of Love

I went to the Garden of Love,
And saw what I never had seen:
A Chapel was built in the midst,
Where I used to play on the green.

And the gates of this Chapel were shut,
And 'Thou shalt not' writ over the door;
So I turn'd to the Garden of Love
That so many sweet flowers bore;

And I saw it was filled with graves,
And tomb-stones where flowers should be;
And Priests in black gowns were walking their rounds,
And binding with briars my joys & desires.

London

I wander through each chartered street,
Near where the chartered Thames does flow,
And mark in every face I meet
Marks of weakness, marks of woe.

In every cry of every man,
In every infant's cry of fear,
In every voice, in every ban,
The mind-forged manacles I hear.

How the chimney-sweeper's cry
Every blackening church appals;
And the hapless soldier's sigh
Runs in blood down palace walls.

But most through midnight streets I hear
How the youthful harlot's curse
Blasts the new-born infant's tear,
And blights with plagues the marriage hearse.

Tiger, Tiger burning bright

Tiger! Tiger! burning bright
In the forests of the night,
What immortal hand or eye
Could frame thy fearful symmetry?

In what distant deeps or skies
Burned the fire of thine eyes?
On what wings dare he aspire?
What the hand dare seize the fire?

And what shoulder, and what art,
Could twist the sinews of thy heart?
And when thy heart began to beat,
What dread hand? And what dread feet?

What the hammer? What the chain?
In what furnace was thy brain?
What the anvil?
What dread grasp
Dare its deadly terrors clasp?

When the stars threw down their spears,
And watered heaven with their tears,
Did he smile his work to see?
Did he who made the Lamb make thee?

Tiger! Tiger! burning bright
In the forests of the night,
What immortal hand or eye
Dare frame thy fearful symmetry?

William Wordsworth (1770-1850)

She was a Phantom of Delight

She was a phantom of delight
When first she gleam'd upon my sight:
A lovely apparition sent
To be a moment's ornament;
Her eyes as stars of twilight fair;
Like Twilight's, too, her dusky hair;
But all things else about her drawn
From May-time and the cheerful dawn;
A Dancing shape, an image gay,
To haunt, to startle, and waylay.

I saw her upon nearer view,
A spirit, yet a woman too!
Her household motions light and free,
And steps of virgin-liberty;
A countenance in which did meet
Sweet records, promises as sweet;
A creature not too bright or good
For human nature's daily food,
For transient sorrows, simple wiles,
Praise, blame, love, kisses, tears, and smiles.

And now I see with eye serene
The very pulse of the machine;
A being breathing thoughtful breath,
A traveller between life and death:
The reason firm, the temperate will,

Endurance, foresight, strength, and skill;
A perfect woman, nobly plann'd
To warn, to comfort, and command;
And yet a Spirit still, and bright
With something of an angel-light.

This excerpt from a longer poem, may tempt you to read the rest.

from Ode : Intimations of Immortality from Recollections of Early Childhood

There was a time when meadow, grove, and stream,
The earth, and every common sight
To me did seem
Apparell'd in celestial light,
The glory and the freshness of a dream.
It is not now as it has been of yore; -
Turn whereso'er I may,
By night or day,
The things which I have seen I now can see no more!
The rainbow comes and goes,
And lovely is the rose;
The moon doth with delight
Look round her when the heavens are bare;
Waters on a starry night
Are beautiful and fair;
The sunshine is a glorious birth;
But yet I know, where'er I go,
That there hath pass'd away a glory from the earth.

Louisa
After accompanying her on a mountain excursion

I met Louisa in the shade,
And, having seen that lovely Maid,
Why should I fear to say
That, nymph-like, she is fleet and strong;
And down the rocks can leap along
Like rivulets in May?

And she hath smiles to earth unknown;
Smiles, that with motion of their own
Do spread, and sink, and rise;
That come and go with endless play,
And ever, as they pass away,
Are hidden in her eyes.

She loves her fire, her cottage-home;
Yet o'er the moorland will she roam
In weather rough and bleak;
And, when against the wind she strains,
Oh! might I kiss the mountain rains
That sparkle on her cheek.

Take all that's mine 'beneath the moon',
If I with her but half a noon
May sit beneath the walls
Of some old cave, or mossy nook,
When up she winds along the brook
To hunt the waterfalls.

Samuel Taylor Coleridge (1772-1834)

Work without Hope

All Nature seems at work. Slugs leave their lair -
The bees are stirring - birds are on the wing -
And Winter, slumbering in the open air,
Wears on his smiling face a dream of Spring!
And I, the while, the sole unbusy thing,
Nor honey make, nor pair, nor build, nor sing.

Yet well I ken the banks where amaranths blow,
Have traced the fount whence streams of nectar flow.
Bloom, O ye amaranths! bloom for whom ye may,
For me ye bloom not! Glide, rich streams away!
With lips unbrightened, wreathless brow, I stroll:
And would you learn the spells that drowse my soul?
Work without Hope draws nectar in a sieve,
And Hope without an object cannot live.

Hunting Song

Up, up! ye dames, and lasses gay!
To the meadows trip away.
'Tis you must tend the flocks this morn,
And scare the small birds from the corn.
Not a soul at home may stay:
For the shepherds must go
With lance and bow
To hunt the wolf in the woods today.

Leave the hearth and leave the house
To the cricket and the mouse:
Find grannam out a sunny seat,
With babe and lambkin at her feet.
Not a soul at home may stay:
For the shepherds must go
With lance and bow
To hunt the wolf in the woods today.

Kubla Khan

In Xanadu did Kubla Khan
A stately pleasure-dome decree:
Where Alph, the sacred river, ran
Through caverns measureless to man
Down to a sunless sea.
So twice five miles of fertile ground
With walls and towers were girdled round:
And here were gardens bright with sinuous rills,

Where blossomed many an incense-bearing tree;
And here were forests ancient as the hills,
Enfolding sunny spots of greenery.

But oh! that deep romantic chasm which slanted
Down the green hill athwart a cedarn cover!
A savage place! as holy and enchanted
As e'er beneath a waning moon was haunted
By woman wailing for her demon-lover!
And from this chasm, with ceaseless turmoil seething
As if this earth in fast thick pants were breathing,
A mighty fountain momently was forced:
Amid whose swift half-intermitted burst
Huge fragments vaulted like rebounding hail
Or chaffy grain beneath the thresher's flail:
And 'mid these dancing rocks at once and ever
It flung up momently the sacred river.
Five miles meandering with a mazy motion
Through wood and dale the sacred river ran,
Then reached the caverns measureless to man,
And sank in tumult to a lifeless ocean:
And 'mid this tumult Kubla heard from far
Ancestral voices prophesying war!

The shadow of the dome of pleasure
Floated midway on the waves;
Where was heard the mingled measure
From the fountain and the caves.
It was a miracle of rare device,
A sunny pleasure-dome with caves of ice!
A damsel with a dulcimer
In a vision once I saw:
It was an Abyssinian maid,
And on her dulcimer she played,

Singing of Mount Abora.
Could I revive within me
Her symphony and song,
To such a deep delight 'twould win me,
That with music loud and long,
I would build that dome in air,
That sunny dome! those caves of ice!
And all who heard should see them there,
And all should cry, Beware! Beware!
His flashing eyes, his floating hair!
Weave a circle round him thrice,
And close your eyes with holy dread,
For he on honey-dew hath fed,
And drunk the milk of Paradise.

Jane Taylor (1783-1824)

Twinkle, twinkle little star

Twinkle, twinkle, little star,
How I wonder what you are.
Up above the world so high,
Like a diamond in the sky.

When the blazing sun is gone,
When he nothing shines upon,
Then you show your little light,
Twinkle, twinkle, all the night.

Then the traveller in the dark,
Thanks you for your tiny spark,
He could not see which way to go,
If you did not twinkle so.

In the dark blue sky you keep,
And often through my curtains peep,
For you never shut your eye,
'Til the sun is in the sky.

As you bright and tiny spark,
Light the traveller in the dark, -
Though I know not what you are,
Twinkle, twinkle, little star.

Percy Bysshe Shelley (1792-1822)

Ode to the West Wind

I

O Wild West Wind, thou breath of Autumn's being,
Thou from whose unseen presence the leaves dead
Are driven like ghosts from an enchanter fleeing,

Yellow, and black, and pale, and hectic red,
Pestilence-stricken multitudes! O thou
Who chariotest to their dark wintry bed

The wingèd seeds, where they lie cold and low,
Each like a corpse within its grave, until
Thine azure sister of the Spring shall blow

Her clarion o'er the dreaming earth, and fill
(Driving sweet buds like flocks to feed in air)
With living hues and odours plain and hill;

Wild Spirit, which art moving everywhere;
 Destroyer and preserver; hear, O hear!

II

Thou on whose stream, 'mid the steep sky's commotion,
Loose clouds like earth's decaying leaves are shed,
Shook from the tangled boughs of heaven and ocean,

Angels of rain and lightning! there are spread
On the blue surface of thine airy surge,
Like the bright hair uplifted from the head

Of some fierce Maenad, even from the dim verge
Of the horizon to the zenith's height,
The locks of the approaching storm, Thou dirge

Of the dying year, to which this closing night
Will be the dome of a vast sepulchre,
Vaulted with all thy congregated might

Of vapours, from whose solid atmosphere
Black rain, and fire, and hail will burst: O hear!

III

Thou who didst waken from his summer dreams
The blue Mediterranean, where he lay,
Lulled by the coil of his crystalline streams,

Beside a pumice isle in Baiae's bay,
And saw in sleep old palaces and towers
Quivering within the wave's intenser day,

All overgrown with azure moss, and flowers
So sweet, the sense faints picturing them! Thou
For whose path the Atlantic's level powers

Cleave themselves into chasms, while far below
The sea-blooms and the oozy woods which wear
The sapless foliage of the ocean, know

Thy voice, and suddenly grow gray with fear,
And tremble and despoil themselves: O hear!

IV

If I were a dead leaf thou mightest bear;
If I were a swift cloud to fly with thee;
A wave to pant beneath thy power, and share

The impulse of thy strength, only less free
Than thou, O uncontrollable! if even
I were as in my boyhood, and could be

The comrade of thy wanderings over heaven,
As then, when to outstrip thy skiey speed
Scarce seemed a vision - I would ne'er have striven

As thus with thee in prayer in my sore need.
O! lift me as a wave, a leaf, a cloud!
I fall upon the thorns of life! I bleed!

A heavy weight of hours has chained and bowed
One too like thee - tameless, and swift, and proud.

V

Make my thy lyre, even as the forest is:
What if my leaves are falling like its own?
The tumult of thy mighty harmonies

Will take from both a deep autumnal tone,
Sweet though in sadness. Be thou, Spirit fierce,
My spirit! Be thou me, impetuous one!

Drive my dead thoughts over the universe,
Like withered leaves, to quicken a new birth;
And, by the incantation of this verse,

Scatter, as from an unextinguished hearth
Ashes and sparks, my words among mankind!
Be through my lips to unawakened earth

The trumpet of a prophecy! O Wind,
If Winter comes, can Spring be far behind?

Love's Philosophy

The fountains mingle with the river
And the rivers with the Ocean,
The winds of Heaven mix for ever
With a sweet emotion;
Nothing in the world is single;
All things by a law divine
In one spirit meet and mingle.
Why not I with thine?-
See the mountains kiss high Heaven
And the waves clasp one another;
No sister-flower would be forgiven
If it disdained its brother;
And the sunlight clasps the earth
And the moonbeams kiss the sea:
What is all this sweet work worth
If thou kiss not me?

To Jane: The Keen Stars Were Twinkling

The keen stars were twinkling,
And the fair moon was rising among them,
Dear Jane!
The guitar was tinkling,
But the notes were not sweet till you sung them
Again.

As the moon's soft splendour
O'er the faint cold starlight of Heaven
Is thrown,
So your voice most tender
To the strings without soul had then given
Its own.

The stars will awaken,
Though the moon sleep a full hour later,
Tonight;
No leaf will be shaken
Whilst the dews of your melody scatter
Delight.

Though the sound overpowers,
Sing again, with your dear voice revealing
A tone
Of some world far from ours,
Where music and moonlight and feeling
Are one.

John Clare (1793-1864)

Little Trotty Wagtail

Little Trotty Wagtail, he went in the rain,
And twittering, tottering sideways, he ne'er got straight again;
He stooped to get a worm, and looked up to get a fly,
And then he flew away ere his feathers they were dry.

Little Trotty Wagtail, he waddled in the mud,
And left his little foot-marks, trample where he would,
He waddled in the water-pudge, and waggle went his tail,
And chirruped up his wings to dry upon the garden rail.

Little Trotty Wagtail, you nimble all about,
And in the dimpling water-pudge you waddle in and out:
Your home is nigh at hand and in the warm pig-stye;
So, little Master Wagtail, I'll bid you a good-bye.

The Vixen

Among the taller wood with ivy hung,
The old fox plays and dances round her young.
She snuffs and barks if any passes by
And swings her tail and turns prepared to fly.
The horseman hurries by, she bolts to see,
And turns agen, from danger never free.
If any stands she runs among the poles
And barks and snaps and drives them in the holes.
The shepherd sees them and the boy goes by
And gets a stick and progs the hole to try.
They get all still and lie in safety sure,
And out again when everything's secure,
And start and snap at blackbirds bouncing by
To fight and catch the great white butterfly.

Autumn

I love the fitful gust that shakes
The casement all the day,
And from the glossy elm-tree takes
The faded leaves away,
Twirling them by the window pane
With thousand others down the lane.

I love to see the shaking twig
Dance till the shut of eve,
The sparrow on the cottage rig,
Whose chirp would make believe
That Spring was just now flirting by
In Summer's lap with flowers to lie.

I love to see the cottage smoke
Curl upwards through the trees,
The pigeons nestled round the cote
On November days like these;
The cock upon the dunghill crowing,
The mill sails on the heath a-going.

The feather from the raven's breast
Falls on the stubble lea,
The acorns near the old crow's nest
Drop pattering down the tree;
The grunting pigs, that wait for all,
Scramble and hurry where they fall.

John Keats (1795-1821)

To Autumn

Season of mists and mellow fruitfulness,
Close bosom-friend of the maturing sun;
Conspiring with him how to load and bless
With fruit the vines that round the thatch-eaves run;
To bend with apples the mossed cottage-trees,
And fill all fruit with ripeness to the core;
To swell the gourd, and plump the hazel shells
With a sweet kernel; to set budding more,
And still more, later flowers for the bees,
Until they think warm days will never cease,
For Summer has o'er-brimmed their clammy cells.

Who hath not seen thee oft amid thy store?
Sometimes whoever seeks abroad may find
Thee sitting careless on a granary floor,
Thy hair soft-lifted by the winnowing wind;
Or on a half-reaped furrow sound asleep,
Drowsed with the fume of poppies, while thy hook
Spares the next swath and all its twinèd flowers:
And sometimes like a gleaner thou dost keep
Steady thy laden head across a brook;
Or by a cider-press, with patient look,
Thou watchest the last oozings hours by hours.

Where are the songs of Spring? Aye, where are they?
Think not of them, thou hast thy music too -
While barrèd clouds bloom the soft-dying day,
And touch the stubble-plains with rosy hue;
Then in a wailful choir the small gnats mourn
Among the river sallows, born aloft
Or sinking as the light wind lives or dies;
And full-grown lambs loud bleat from hilly bourn;
Hedge crickets sing, and now with treble soft
The redbreast whistles from a garden-croft;
And gathering swallows twitter in the skies.

On First Looking into Chapman's Homer

Much have I travelled in the realms of gold,
And many goodly states and kingdoms seen;
Round many western islands have I been
Which bards in fealty to Apollo hold.
Oft of one wide expanse had I been told
That deep-browed Homer ruled as his demesne;
Yet did I never breathe its pure serene
Till I heard Chapman speak out loud and bold:
Then felt I like some watcher of the skies
When a new planet swims into his ken;
Or like stout Cortez when with eagle eyes
He stared at the Pacific - and all his men
Looked at each other with a wild surmise -
Silent, upon a peak in Darien.

Song

O blush not so! O blush not so!
Or I shall think you knowing;
And if you smile the blushing while,
Then maidenheads are going.

There's a blush for won't, and a blush for shan't,
And a blush for having done it:
There's a blush for thought, and a blush for naught,
And a blush for just begun it.

O sigh not so! O sigh not so!
For it sounds of Eve's sweet pippin,
By those loosened lips you have tasted the pips
And fought in an amorous nipping.

Will you play once more at nice-cut-core,
For it only will last our youth out?
And we have the prime of the kissing time,
We have not one sweet tooth out.

There's a sigh for yes, and a sigh for no,
And a sigh for I can't bear it!
O what can be done, shall we stay or run?
O, cut the sweet apple and share it!

Sara Coleridge (1802-1850)

January Brings the Snow

January brings the snow,
Makes our feet and fingers glow.
February brings the rain,
Thaws the frozen lake again.
March brings breezes loud and shrill,
Stirs the dancing daffodil.
April brings the primrose sweet,
Scatters daisies at our feet.
May brings flocks of pretty lambs,
Skipping by their fleecy dams.
June brings tulips, lilies, roses,
Fills the children's hands with posies.
Hot July brings cooling showers,
Apricots and gilly flowers.
August brings the sheaves of corn,
Then the harvest home is borne.
Warm September brings the fruit,
Sportsmen then begin to shoot.
Fresh October brings the pheasant,
Then to gather nuts is pleasant.
Dull November brings the blast,
Then the leaves are whirling fast.
Chill December brings the sleet,
Blazing fire, and Christmas treat.

The Mother

Full oft beside some gorgeous fane
The youngling heifer bleeds and dies;
Her life-blood issuing forth amain,
While wreaths of incense climb the skies.

The mother wanders all around,
Thro' shadowy grove and lightsome glade;
Her footmarks on the yielding ground
Will prove what anxious quest she made.

The stall where late her darling lay
She visits oft with eager look;
In restless movements wastes the day,
And gills with cries each neighb'ring nook.

She roams along the willowy copse,
Where purest waters softly gleam;
But ne'er a leaf or blade she crops,
Nor couches by the gliding stream.

No youthful kine, thro' fresh and fair,
Her vainly searching eyes engage;
No pleasant fields relieve her care,
No murmuring streams her grief assuage.

Trees

The Oak is called the king of trees,
The Aspen quivers in the breeze,
The Poplar grows up straight and tall,
The Peach tree spreads along the wall,
The Sycamore gives pleasant shade,
The Willow droops in watery glade,
The Fir tree useful timber gives,
The Beech amid the forest lives.

Elizabeth Barratt Browning (1806-1861)

A Musical Instrument

What was he doing, the great god Pan.
Down in the reeds by the river?
Spreading ruin and scattering ban,
Splashing and paddling with hoofs of a goat,
And breaking the golden lilies afloat
With the dragon-fly on the river.

He tore out a reed, the great god Pan.
From the deep cool bed of the river:
The limpid water turbidly ran.
And the broken lilies a-dying lay,
And the dragon-fly had fled away,
Ere he brought it out of the river.

High on the shore sat the great god Pan.
While turbidly flowed the river;
And hacked and hewed as a great god can,
With his hard bleak steel at the patient reed,
Till there was not a sign of a leaf indeed
To prove it fresh from the river.

He cut it short, did the great god Pan
(How tall it stood in the river!),
Then drew the pith, like the heart of a man,
Steadily from the outside ring,
And notched the poor dry empty thing
In holes, as he sat by the river.

'This is the way', laughed the great god Pan,
(Laughed while he sat by the river),
'The only way, since gods began
To make sweet music, they could succeed.'
Then, dropping his mouth to a hole in the reed,
He blew in power by the river.

Sweet, sweet, sweet, O Pan!
Piercing sweet by the river!
Blinding sweet, O great god Pan!
The sun on the hill forgot to die,
And the lilies revived, and the dragon-fly
Came back to dream on the river.

Yet half a beast is the great god Pan,
To laugh as he sits by the river.
Making a poet out of a man;
The true gods sigh for the cost and pain -
For the reed which grows nevermore again
As a reed with the reeds in the river.

Grief

I tell you hopeless grief is passionless,
That only men incredulous of despair,
Half-taught in anguish, through the midnight air
Beat upward to God's throne in loud access
Of shrieking and reproach. Full desertness
In souls, as countries, lieth silent-bare
Under the blanching, vertical eye-glare
Of the absolute heavens. Deep-hearted man, express
Grief for thy dead in silence like to death -
Most like a monumental statue set
In everlasting watch and moveless woe
Till itself crumble to the dust beneath.
Touch it; the marble eyelids are not wet
If it could weep, it could arise and go.

A Man's Requirements

I

Love me Sweet, with all thou art,
   Feeling, thinking, seeing;
Love me in the lightest part,
   Love me in full being.

II

Love me with thine open youth
   In its frank surrender;
With the vowing of thy mouth,
   With its silence tender.

III

Love me with thine azure eyes,
   Made for earnest granting;
Taking colour from the skies
   Can Heaven's truth be wanting?

IV

Love me with their lids, that fall
   Snow-like at first meeting;
Love me with thine heart, that all
   Neighbours then see beating.

V

Love me with thine hand stretched out
   Freely - open-minded:
Love me with thy loitering foot, -
   Hearing one behind it.

VI

Love me with thy voice, that turns
   Sudden faint above me;
Love me with thy blush that burns
   When I murmur *Love me!*

VII

Love me with thy thinking soul,
   Break it to love-sighing;
Love me with thy thoughts that roll
   On through living - dying.

VIII

Love me in thy gorgeous airs,
   When the world has crowned thee
Love me, kneeling at thy prayers;
   With the angels round thee.

IX

Love me pure, as musers do.
   Up the woodlands shady:
Love me gaily, fast and true,
   As a winsome lady.

X

Through all hopes that keep us brave
   Farther off or nigher,
Love me for the house and grave,
   And for something higher.

XI

Thus, if thou wilt prove me, Dear,
   Woman's love no fable,
I will love *thee* - half a year -
   As a man is able.

Alfred, Lord Tennyson (1809-1892)

The Miller's Daughter

It is the miller's daughter,
And she is grown so dear, so dear,
That I would be the jewel
That trembles at her ear:
For hid in ringlets day and night,
I'd touch her neck so warm and white.

And I would be the girdle
About her dainty, dainty waist,
And her heart would beat against me,
In sorrow and in rest:
And I should know if it beat right,
I'd clasp it round so close and tight.

And I would be the necklace,
And all day long to fall and rise
Upon her balmy bosom,
With her laughter or her sighs:
And I would lie so light, so light,
I scarce should be unclasped at night.

Many of our favourite verses by Tennyson are excerpts from longer poems, here are two:

from: The Princess: Tears, Idle Tears

Tears, idle tears, I know not what they mean,
Tears from the depth of some divine despair
Rise in the heart, and gather to the eyes,
In looking on the happy autumn-fields,
And thinking of the days that are no more.

Fresh as the first beam glittering on a sail,
That brings our friends up from the underworld,
Sad as the last which reddens over one
That sinks with all we love below the verge;
So sad, so fresh, the days that are no more.

Ah, sad and strange as in dark summer dawns
The earliest pipe of half-awakened birds
To dying ears, when unto dying eyes
The casement slowly grows a glimmering square;
So sad, so strange, the days that are no more.

Dear as remembered kisses after death,
And sweet as those by hopeless fancy feigned
On lips that are for others; deep as love,
Deep as first love, and wild with all regret:
O Death in Life, the days that are no more!

from: The Brook

I come from haunts of coot and hern,
I make a sudden sally
And sparkle out among the fern,
To bicker down a valley.

By thirty hills I hurry down,
Or slip between the ridges,
By twenty thorps, a little town,
And half a hundred bridges.

Till last by Philip's farm I flow
To join the brimming river,
For men may come and men may go,
But I go on for ever.

I chatter over stony ways,
In little sharps and trebles,
I bubble into eddying bays,
I babble on the pebbles.

With many a curve my banks I fret
By many a field and fallow,
And many a fairy foreland set
With willow-weed and mallow.

I chatter, chatter, as I flow
To join the brimming river,
For men may come and men may go
But I go on for ever.

Robert Browning (1812-1889)

Pippa's Song

The year's at the spring
And day's at the morn;
Morning's at seven;
The hill-side's dew-pearled;
The lark's on the wing;
The snail's on the thorn;
God's in his heaven
All's right with the world!

My Last Duchess

SCENE : FERRARA

That's my last Duchess painted on the wall,
Looking as if she were alive. I call
That piece a wonder, now: Fra Pandolf's hands
Worked busily a day, and there she stands.
Will't please you sit and look at her? I said
"Fra Pandolf" by design, for never read
Strangers like you that pictured countenance,
The depth and passion of its earnest glance,
But to myself they turned (since none puts by
The curtain I have drawn for you, but I)
And seemed as they would ask me, if they durst,
How such a glance there; so, not the first

Are you to turn and ask thus. Sir, 'twas not
Her husband's presence only, called that spot
Of joy into the Duchess' cheek: perhaps
Fra Pandolf chanced to say "Her mantle laps
Over my Lady's wrist too much," or "Paint
Must never hope to reproduce the faint
Half-flush that dies along her throat"; such stuff
Was courtesy, she thought, and cause enough
For calling up that spot of joy. She had
A heart... how shall I say?... too soon made glad,
Too easily impressed; she liked whate'er
She looked on, and her looks went everywhere.
Sir, 'twas all one! My favour at her breast,
The drooping of the daylight in the West,
The bough of cherries some officious fool
Broke in the orchard for her, the white mule
She rode with round the terrace - all and each
Would draw from her alike the approving speech,
Or blush, at least. She thanked men, - good; but thanked
Somehow . . . I know not how . . . as if she ranked
My gift of a nine hundred years old name
With anybody's gift. Who'd stoop to blame
This sort of trifling? Even had you skill
In speech - (which I have not) - to make your will
Quite clear to such an one, and say "Just this
Or that in you disgusts me; here you miss,
Or there exceed the mark"- and if she let
Herself be lessoned so, nor plainly set
Her wits to yours, forsooth, and made excuse,
- E'en then would be some stooping, and I choose
Never to stoop. Oh, Sir, she smiled, no doubt,
Whene'er I passed her; but who passed without
Much the same smile? This grew; I gave commands;
Then all smiles stopped together. There she stands

As if alive. Will't please you rise? We'll meet
The company below, then. I repeat,
The Count your Master's known munificence
Is ample warrant that no just pretence
Of mine for dowry will be disallowed;
Though his fair daughter's self, as I avowed
At starting, is my object. Nay, we'll go
Together down, Sir! Notice Neptune, tho',
Taming a sea-horse, thought a rarity,
Which Claus of Innsbruck cast in bronze for me.

from: *The Pied Piper*

The Pied Piper is another very long poem - here are three representative extracts, but if you read the whole poem, you may choose some other verses.

1. Hamelin Town's in Brunswick,
   By famous Hanover city;
   The river Weser, deep and wide,
   Washes its wall on the southern side;
   A pleasanter spot you never spied;
   But, when begins my ditty,
   Almost five hundred years ago,
   To see the townsfolk suffer so
   From vermin, was a pity.

Rats!
They fought the dogs, and killed the cats,
And bit the babies in the cradles,
And ate the cheeses out of the vats,
And licked the soup from the cooks' own ladles,
Split open the kegs of salted sprats,
Made nests inside men's Sunday hats,
And even spoiled the women's chats,
By drowning their speaking
With shrieking and squeaking
In fifty different sharps and flats.

At last the people in a body
To the Town Hall came flocking:
''Tis clear,' cried they, 'our Mayor's a noddy;
And as for our Corporation - shocking
To think we buy gowns lined with ermine
For dolts that can't or won't determine
What's best to rid us of our vermin!
You hope, because you're old and obese,
To find in the furry civic robe ease?
Rouse up, Sirs! Give your brains a racking
To find the remedy we're lacking,
Or, sure as fate, we'll send you packing!'
At this the Mayor and Corporation
Quaked with a mighty consternation.

2. Into the streets the Piper stept,
   Smiling first a little smile,
   As if he knew what magic slept
   In his quiet pipe the while;
   Then, like a musical adept,
   To blow the pipe his lips he wrinkled,
   And green and blue his sharp eyes twinkled

Like a candle-flame where salt is sprinkled;
And ere three shrill notes the pipe uttered,
You heard as if an army muttered;
And the muttering grew to a grumbling;
And the grumbling grew to a mighty rumbling;
And out of the houses the rats came tumbling.
Great rats, small rats, lean rats, brawny rats,
Brown rats, black rats, grey rats, tawny rats,
Grave old plodders, gay young friskers,
Fathers, mothers, uncles, cousins,
Cocking tails and pricking whiskers,
Families by tens and dozens,
Brothers, sisters, husbands, wives -
Followed the Piper for their lives.
From street to street he piped advancing,
And step for step they followed dancing,
Until they came to the river Weser
Wherein all plunged and perished!
Save one who, stout as Julius Caesar,
Swam across and lived to carry
(As he, the manuscript he cherished)
To Rat-land home his commentary:
Which was, 'At the first shrill notes of the pipe,
I heard a sound as of scraping tripe,
And putting apples, wondrous ripe,
Into a cider-press's gripe:
And a moving away of pickle-tub-boards,
And a leaving ajar of conserve-cupboards,
And a drawing the corks of train-oil-flasks,
And a breaking the hoops of butter-casks;
And it seemed as if a voice
(Sweeter far than by harp or by psaltery
Is breathed) called out, Oh rats, rejoice!
The world is grown to one vast dry-saltery!

So, munch on, crunch on, take your nuncheon,
Breakfast, supper, dinner, luncheon!
And just as a bulky sugar-puncheon,
All ready staved, like a great sun shone
Glorious scarce an inch before me,
Just as methought it said, Come, bore me!
- I found the Weser rolling o'er me.'

3. Alas, alas for Hamelin!
There came into many a burgher's pate
A text which says that Heaven's Gate
Opes to the Rich at as easy rate
As the needle's eye takes a camel in!
The Mayor sent East, West, North and South,
To offer the Piper, by word of mouth,
Wherever it was men's lot to find him,
Silver and gold to his heart's content,
If he'd only return the way he went,
And bring the children behind him.
But when they saw 'twas a lost endeavour,
And Piper and dancers were gone for ever,
They made a decree that lawyers never
Should think their records dated duly
If, after the day of the month and year,
These words did not as well appear,
'And so long after what happened here
On the Twenty-second of Júly,
Thirteen hundred and seventy-six:'
And the better in memory to fix
The place of the children's last retreat,
They called it, the Pied Piper's Street -
Where any one playing on pipe or tabor
Was sure for the future to lose his labour.
Nor suffered they hostelry or tavern

To shock with mirth a street so solemn;
But opposite the place of the cavern
They wrote the story on a column,
And on the great Church-Window painted
The same, to make the world acquainted
How their children were stolen away;
And there it stands to this very day.
And I must not omit to say
That in Transylvania there's a tribe
Of alien people that ascribe
The outlandish ways and dress
On which their neighbours lay such stress,
To their fathers and mothers having risen
Out of some subterraneous prison
Into which they were trepanned
Long time ago in a mighty band
Out of Hamelin town in Brunswick land,
But how or why, they don't understand.
So, Willy, let me and you be wipers
Of scores out with all men - especially pipers:
And, whether they pipe us free, from rats or from mice,
If we've promised them aught, let us keep our promise.

Charles Kingsley (1819-1875)

Three Fishers went Sailing

Three fishers went sailing out into the West,
Away to the West as the sun went down;
Each thought on the woman who loved him the best,
And the children stood watching them out of the town:
For men must work, and women must weep,
And there's little to earn, and many to keep,
Though the harbour-bar be moaning.

Three wives sat up in the lighthouse tower,
And they trimm'd the lamps as the sun went down;
And they looked at the squall, and they looked at the shower,
And the night-rack came rolling up ragged and brown;
But men must work, and women must weep,
Though storms be sudden, and waters deep,
And the harbour-bar be moaning.

Three corpses lay out on the shining sands,
In the morning gleam, as the tide went down,
And the women are weeping and wringing their hands,
For those who will never come home to the town.
For men must work, and women must weep,
And the sooner it's over, the sooner to sleep,
And good-bye to the bar and its moaning.

A Farewell

My fairest child, I have no song to give you;
No lark could pipe in skies so dull and grey;
Yet, if you will, one quiet hint I'll leave you,
For every day.

I'll tell you how to sing a clearer carol
Than lark who hails the dawn on breezy down;
To earn yourself a purer poet's laurel
Than Shakespeare's crown.

Be good, sweet maid, and let who can be clever;
Do noble things, not dream them, all day long;
And so make Life, Death and that last For Ever,
One grand sweet song.

The Sands of Dee

'O Mary, go and call the cattle home,
And call the cattle home,
And call the cattle home
Across the sands of Dee';
The western wind was wild and dank with foam,
And all alone went she.

The western tide crept up along the sand,
And o'er and o'er the sand,
And round and round the sand,
As far as eye could see.
The rolling mist came down and hid the land:
And never home came she.

'Oh! is it weed, or fish, or floating hair -
A tress of golden hair,
A drownèd maiden's hair
Above the nets at sea?
Was never salmon yet that shone so fair
Among the stakes on Dee.'

They rowed her in across the rolling foam,
The cruel crawling foam,
The cruel hungry foam,
To her grave beside the sea:
But still the boatmen hear her call the cattle home
Across the sands of Dee.

Matthew Arnold (1822-1888)

Dover Beach

The sea is calm to-night.
The tide is full, the moon lies fair
Upon the straits - on the French coast, the light
Gleams, and is gone; the cliffs of England stand,
Glimmering and vast, out in the tranquil bay.
Come to the window, sweet is the night air!
Only, from the long line of spray
Where the sea meets the moon-blanched sand,
Listen! you hear the grating roar
Of pebbles which the waves suck back, and fling,
At their return, up the high strand,
Begin, and cease, and then again begin,
With tremulous cadence slow, and bring
The eternal note of sadness in.

Sophocles long ago
Heard it on the Ægæan, and it brought
Into his mind the turbid ebb and flow.
Of human misery; we
Find also in the sound a thought,
Hearing it by this distant northern sea.

The sea of faith
Was once, too, at the full, and round earth's shore
Lay like the folds of a bright girdle furled;
But now I only hear
Its melancholy, long, withdrawing roar,
Retreating to the breath
Of the night-wind down the vast edges drear
And naked shingles of the world.

Ah, love, let us be true
To one another! for the world, which seems
To lie before us like a land of dreams,
So various, so beautiful, so new,
Hath really neither joy, nor love, nor light,
Nor certitude, nor peace, nor help for pain;
And we are here as on a darkling plain
Swept with confused alarms of struggle and flight,
Where ignorant armies clash by night.

Philomela

Hark, ah, the nightingale -
The tawny-throated!
Hark, from that moonlit cedar what a burst!
What triumph! hark! - what pain!

O wanderer from a Grecian shore,
Still, after many years, in distant lands,
Still nourishing in thy bewildered brain
That wild, unquenched, deep-sunken old-world pain -
Say, will it never heal?
And can this fragrant lawn
With its cool trees, and night,
And the sweet , tranquil Thames,
And moonshine, and the dew,
To thy racked heart and brain
Afford no balm?

Dost thou to-night behold,
Here, through the moonlight on this English grass,
The unfriendly palace in the Thracian wild?
Dost thou again peruse
With hot cheeks and seared eyes
The too clear web, and thy dumb sister's shame?
Dost thou once assay
Thy flight, and feel come over thee,
Poor fugitive, the feathery change

Once more, and once more seem to make resound
With love and hate, triumph and agony,
Lone Daulis, and the high Cephissian vale?
Listen, Eugenia -
How thick the bursts come crowding through the leaves!
Again - thou hearest?
Eternal passion!
Eternal pain!

Requiescat

Strew on her roses, roses,
And never a spray of yew!
In quiet she reposes;
Ah, would that I did too!

Her mirth the world required;
She bathed it in smiles of glee.
But her heart was tired, tired,
And now they let her be.

Her life was turning, turning,
In mazes of heat and sound.
But for peace her soul was yearning,
And now peace laps her round.

Her cabined, ample spirit,
It fluttered and failed for breath.
To-night it doth inherit
The vasty hall of death.

Emily Dickinson (1830-1886)

Because I could not stop for Death

Because I could not stop for Death -
He kindly stopped for me -
The Carriage held but just Ourselves -
And Immortality.

We slowly drove - He knew no haste
And I had put away
My labor and my leisure too,
For His Civilty -

We passed the School, where Children strove
At Recess - in the Ring -
We passed the Fields of Gazing Grain -
We passed the Setting Sun -

Or rather - He passed Us -
The Dews drew quivering and chill -
For only Gossamer, my Gown -
My Tippet - only Tulle -

We paused before a House that seemed
A Swelling of the Ground -
The Roof was scarcely visible -
The Cornice - in the Ground -

Since then - 'tis Centuries - and yet
Feels shorter than the Day
I first surmised the Horses' Heads
Were toward Eternity -

The Waking Year

A Lady red upon the hill
Her annual secret keeps;
A lady white within the field
In placid lily sleeps!

The tidy breezes with their brooms
Sweep vale, and hill, and tree!
Prithee, my pretty housewives!
Who may expected be?

The neighbours do not yet suspect!
The woods exchange a smile, -
Orchard, and buttercup, and bird,
In such a little while!

And yet how still the landscape stands,
How nonchalant the wood,
As if the resurrection
Were nothing very odd!

Like Rain it sounded till it curved

Like Rain it sounded till it curved
And then I knew 'twas Wind -
It walked as wet as any Wave
But swept as dry as sand -
When it had pushed itself away
To some remotest Plain
A coming as of Hosts was heard
That was indeed the Rain -
It filled the Wells, it pleased the Pools
It warbled in the Road -
It pulled the spigot from the Hills
And let the Floods abroad -
It loosened acres, lifted seas
The sites of Centres stirred
Then like Elijah rode away
Upon a Wheel of Cloud.

Christina Rossetti (1830-1894)

The Wind

Who has seen the wind?
Neither I nor you;
But when the leaves hang trembling
The wind is passing through.

Who has seen the wind?
Neither you nor I;
But when the trees bow down their heads
The wind is passing by.

Song

When I am dead, my dearest,
Sing no sad songs for me;
Plant thou no roses at my head,
Nor shady cypress tree:
Be the green grass above me
With showers and dewdrops wet;
And if thou wilt, remember,
And if thou wilt, forget.

I shall not see the shadows,
I shall not feel the rain;
I shall not hear the nightingale
Sing on, as if in pain:
And dreaming through the twilight
That doth not rise nor set,
Haply I may remember,
And haply may forget.

The following extracts from "Goblin Market" will, we hope, whet your appetite to read the whole poem and make you own selection.

from: Goblin Market

1. Morning and evening
   Maids heard the goblins cry:
   'Come buy our orchard fruits,
   Come buy, come buy:
   Apples and quinces,
   Lemons and oranges,
   Plump unpecked cherries,
   Melons and raspberries,
   Bloom-down-checked peaches,
   Swart-headed mulberries,
   Wild free-born cranberries,
   Crab-apples, dewberries,
   Pine-apples, blackberries,
   Apricots, strawberries; -
   All ripe together
   In summer weather, -
   Morns that pass by,
   Fair eves that fly;

Come buy, come buy:
Our grapes fresh from the vine,
Pomegranates full and fine,
Dates and sharp bullaces,
Rare pears and greengages,
Damsons and bilberries,
Taste them and try:
Currants and gooseberries,
Bright-fire like barberries,
Figs to fill your mouth,
Citrons from the South,
Sweet to tongue and sound to eye;
Come buy, come buy.'

Evening by evening
 Among the brookside rushes,
Laura bowed her head to hear,
Lizzie veiled her blushes:
Crouching close together
In the cooling weather,
With clasping arms and cautioning lips,
With tingling cheeks and finger tips.
'Lie close,' Laura said,
Pricking up her golden head:
'We must not look at goblin men,
We must not buy their fruits:
Who knows upon what soil they fed
 Their hungry thirsty roots?'
'Come buy', call the goblins
 Hobbling down the glen.
'Oh,' cried Lizzie, 'Laura, Laura,
 You should not peep at goblin men.'
 Lizzie covered up her eyes,
 Covered close lest they should look;

      Laura reared her glossy head,
      And whispered like the restless brook:
      'Look, Lizzie, look, Lizzie,
      Down the glen tramp little men.'

2.   But sweet-tooth Laura spoke in haste:
      'Good folk, I have no coin;
      To take were to purloin:
      I have no copper in my purse,
      I have no silver either,
      And all my gold is on the furze
      That shakes in windy weather
      Above the rusty heather.'
      'You have much gold upon your head.'
      They answered all together:
      'Buy from us with a golden curl.'
      She clipped a precious golden lock,
      She dropped a tear more than pearl,
      Then sucked their fruit globes fair or red:
      Sweeter than honey from the rock,
      Stronger than man-rejoicing wine,
      Clearer than water flowed that juice;
      She never tasted such before,
      How should it cloy with length of use?
      She sucked and sucked and sucked the more
      Fruits which that unknown orchard bore;
      She sucked until her lips were sore;
      Then flung the emptied rinds away
      But gathered up one kernel stone,
      And knew not was it night or day
      As she turned home alone.

      Lizzie met her at the gate
      Full of wise upbraidings:
      'Dear, you should not stay so late,

Twilight is not good for maidens;
Should not loiter in the glen
In the haunts of goblin men.
Do you not remember Jeanie,
How she met them in the moonlight,
Took their gifts both choice and many,
Ate their fruits and wore their flowers
Plucked from bowers
Where summer ripens at all hours?
But ever in the moonlight
She pined and pined away;
Sought them by night and day,
Found them no more but dwindled and grew grey;
Then fell with the first snow,
While to this day no grass will grow
Where she lies low:
I planted daisies there a year ago
That never blow.
You should not loiter so.'
'Nay, hush,' said Laura:
'Nay, hush, my sister:
I ate and ate my fill,
Yet my mouth waters still;
To-morrow night I will
Buy more': and kissed her:
'Have done with sorrow;
I'll bring you plums to-morrow
Fresh on their mother twigs,
Cherries worth getting;
You cannot think what figs
My teeth have met in,
What melons icy-cold
Piled on a dish of gold
Too huge for me to hold.

3. Swift fire spread through her veins, knocked at her heart,
   Met the fire smouldering there
   And overbore its lesser flame;
   She gorged on bitterness without a name:
   Ah! fool, to choose such part
   Of soul-consuming care!
   Sense failed in the mortal strife:
   Like the watch-tower of a town
   Which an earthquake shatters down,
   Like a lighting-stricken mast,
   Like a wind-uprooted tree
   Spun about,
   Like a foam-topped waterspout
   Cast down headlong in the sea,
   She fell at last;
   Pleasure past and anguish past,
   Is it death or is it life?

   Life out of death.
   That night long Lizzie watched by her,
   Counted her pulse's flagging stir,
   Felt for her breath,
   Held water to her lips, and cooled her face
   With tears and fanning leaves:
   But when the first birds chirped about their eaves,
   And early reapers plodded to the place
   Of golden sheaves,
   And dew-wet grass
   Bowed in the morning winds so brisk to pass,
   And new buds with new day
   Opened of cup-like lilies on the stream,
   Laura awoke as from a dream,
   Laughed in the innocent old way,
   Hugged Lizzie but not twice or thrice;
   Her gleaming locks showed not one thread of grey,

Her breath was sweet as May
And light danced in her eyes.

Days, weeks, months, years
Afterwards, when both were wives
With children of their own;
Their mother-hearts beset with fears,
Their lives bound up in tender lives;
Laura would call the little ones
And tell them of her early prime,
Those pleasant days long gone
of not-returning time:
Would talk about the haunted glen,
The wicked, quaint fruit-merchant men,
Their fruits like honey to the throat
But poison in the blood;
(Men sell not such in any town:)
Would tell them how her sister stood
In deadly peril to do her good,
And win the fiery antidote:
Then joining hands to little hands
Would bid them cling together,
'For there is no friend like a sister
In calm or stormy weather;
To cheer one on the tedious way,
To fetch one if one goes astray,
To lift one if one totters down,
To strengthen whilst one stands.'

Uphill

Does the road wind uphill all the way?
Yes, to the very end.
Will the day's journey take the whole long day?
From morn to night, my friend.

But is there for the night a resting-place?
A roof for when the slow, dark hours begin.
May not the darkness hide it from my face?
You cannot miss that inn.
Shall I meet other wayfarers at night?
Those who have gone before.
Then must I knock, or call when just in sight?
They will not keep you waiting at that door.

Shall I find comfort, travel-sore and weak?
Of labour you shall find the sum.
Will there be beds for me and all who seek?
Yea, beds for all who come.

Remember

Remember me when I am gone away,
Gone far away into the silent land;
When you can no more hold me by the hand,
Nor I half turn to go, yet turning stay.
Remember me when no more day by day
You tell me of our future that you plann'd:
Only remember me; you understand
It will be late to counsel then or pray.
Yet if you should forget me for a while
And afterwards remember, do not grieve:
For if the darkness and corruption leave
A vestige of the thoughts that once I had,
Better by far you should forget and smile
Than that you should remember and be sad.

Laurence Alma Tadema
(1836-1912)

Little Girls

If no one ever marries me, -
And I don't see why they should,
For nurse says I'm not pretty,
And I'm seldom very good -

If no one ever marries me
I shan't mind very much,
I shall buy a squirrel in a cage,
And a little rabbit-hutch;

I shall have a cottage near a wood,
And a pony all my own,
And a little lamb, quite clean and tame,
That I can take to town;

And when I'm getting really old, -
At twenty eight or nine -
I shall buy a little orphan girl
And bring her up as mine.

Alice Meynell (1847-1922)

The Rainy Summer

There's much afoot in heaven and earth this year;
The winds hunt up the sun, hunt up the moon,
Trouble the dubious dawn, hasten the drear
Height of a threatening noon.

No breath of boughs, no breath of leaves, of fronds,
May linger or grow warm; the trees are loud;
The forest, rooted, tosses in her bonds,
And strains against the cloud.

No scents may pause within the garden-fold;
The rifled flowers are cold as ocean-shells;
Bees, humming in the storm, carry their cold
Wild honey to cold cells.

In Manchester Square
In Memoriam T.H.

The paralytic man has dropped in death
The crossing-sweeper's brush to which he clung,
One-handed, twisted, dwarfed, scanted of breath,
Although his hair was young.

I saw this year the winter vines of France,
Dwarfed, twisted goblins in the frosty drouth -
Gnarled, crippled, blackened little stems askance
On long hills to the South.

Great green and golden hands of leaves ere long
Shall proffer clusters in that vineyard wide.
And O his might, his sweet, his wine, his song,
His stature, since he died!

A Thrush before Dawn

A voice peals in this end of night
A phrase of notes resembling stars,
Single and spiritual notes of light.
What call they at my window-bars?
The South, the past, the day to be,
An ancient infelicity.

Darkling, deliberate, what sings
This wonderful one, alone, at peace?
What wilder things than song, what things
Sweeter than youth, clearer than Greece,
Dearer than Italy, untold
Delight, and freshness centuries old?

And first first-loves, a multitude,
The exaltation of their pain;
Ancestral childhood long renewed;
And midnights of invisible rain;
And gardens, gardens, night and day,
Gardens and childhood all the way.

What Middle Ages passionate,
O passionless voice! What distant bells
Lodged in the hills, what palace state
Illyrian! For it speaks, it tells,
Without desire, without dismay,
Some morrow and some yesterday.

All-natural things! But more - Whence came
This yet remoter mystery?
How do these starry notes proclaim
A graver still divinity?
This hope, this sancity of fear?
O innocent throat! O human ear!

Edith Nesbit (1858-1924)

Child's Song in Spring

The silver birch is a dainty lady,
She wears a satin gown;
The elm tree makes the old churchyard shady,
She will not live in town.

The English oak is a sturdy fellow,
He gets his green coat late;
The willow is smart in a suit of yellow,
While brown the beech trees wait.

Such a gay green gown God gives the larches -
As green as He is good!
The hazels hold up their arms for arches
When Spring rides through the wood.

The chestnut's proud and the lilac's pretty,
The poplar's gentle and tall,
But the plane tree's kind to the poor dull city -
I love him best of all!

In the Cabinet Drawer

With the amethyst necklace she carried,
Laid by with the scraps of her lace;
And the bonnet she wore to be married,
My young mother's face.

The very same bonnet looms large in
The photograph's yellowish shade,
With 'Studio' below in the margin,
'Smith, Brighton Parade'.

There's the smile the photographer ordered,
The dear little head tilted back;
The dress was a lilac, and bordered
With patterns in black.

It was crinoline-time, and they trimmed it
With terrible trimmings of gimp;
How quaint! It's my tears that have dimmed it -
The border is limp.

She was but a child when she married,
And younger than I when she died;
And here is the rose that she carried
When she was a bride.

For the touch of my fingers upon it,
The print of my tears and my kiss
On the bright little face in the bonnet -
Time leaves me but this!

Baby's Birthday
G.T.A.

Before your life that is to come,
Love stands with eager eyes, that vainly
Seek to discern what gift may fit
The slow unfolding years of it;
And still Time's lips are sealed and dumb,
And still Love no future plainly.

We cannot guess what flowers will spring
Best in your garden, bloom most brightly;
But some fair flowers in any plot
Will spring and grow, and wither not;
And such wish-flowers we gladly bring,
And in that small hand lay them lightly.

Baby, we wish that those dear eyes
May see fulfilment of our dreaming,
Those little feet may turn from wrong,
Those hands to hold the right be strong,
That heart be pure, that mind be wise
To know the true from the true-seeming.

We wish that all your life may be
A life of selfless brave endeavour -
That for reward the fates allow
Such love as lines your soft nest now
To warm the years for you, when we,
Who wish you this, are cold for ever.

Rupert Brooke (1887-1915)

The Soldier

If I should die, think only this of me:
That there's some corner of a foreign field
That is for ever England. There shall be
In that rich earth a richer dust conceal'd;
A dust whom England bore, shaped, made aware,
Gave, once, her flowers to love, her ways to roam,
A body of England's, breathing English air.
Wash'd by the rivers, blest by suns of home.
And think, this heart, all evil shed away,
A pulse in the eternal mind, no less
Gives somewhere back the thoughts by England given;
Her sights and sounds; dreams happy as her day;
And laughter, learnt of friends; and gentleness,
In hearts at peace, under an English heaven.

Clouds

Down the blue night the unending columns press
In noiseless tumult, break and wave and flow,
Now tread the far South, or lift rounds of snow
Up to the white moon's hidden loveliness.

Some pause in their grave wandering comradeless,
And turn with profound gesture vague and slow,
As who would pray good for the world, but know
Their benediction empty as they bless.

They say that the Dead die not, but remain
Near to the rich heirs of their grief and mirth.
I think they ride the calm mid-heaven, as these,
In wise majestic melancholy train,
And watch the moon, and the still-raging seas,
And men, coming and going on the earth.

Wilfred Owen (1893-1918)

Futility

Move him into the sun -
Gently its touch awoke him once,
At home, whispering of fields unsown
Always it woke him, even in France,
Until this morning and this snow.
If anything might rouse him now
The kind old sun will know.

Think how it wakes the seeds, -
Woke, once, the clays of a cold star.
Are limbs, so dear-achieved, are sides,
Full-nerved - still warm - too hard to stir
Was it for this the clay grew tall?
- O what made fatuous sunbeams toil
To break earth's sleep at all?

The Send-Off

Down the close, darkening lanes they sang their way
To the siding-shed,
And lined the train with faces grimly gay.

Their breasts were struck all white with wreath and spray
As men's are, dead.

Dull porters watched them, and a casual tramp
Stood staring hard,
Sorry to miss them from the upland camp.
Then, unmoved, signals nodded, and a lamp
Winked to the guard.

So secretly, like wrongs hushed-up, they went.
They were not ours:
We never heard to which front these were sent.

Nor there if they yet mock what women meant
Who gave them flowers.

Shall they return to beatings of great bells
In wild train-loads?
A few, a few, too few for drums and yells,
May creep back, silent, to village wells
Up half-known roads.

Greater Love

Red lips are not so red
As the stained stones kissed by the English dead.
Kindness of wooed and wooer
Seems shame to their love pure.
O Love, your eyes lose lure
When I behold eyes blinded in my stead!

Your slender attitude
Trembles not exquisite like limbs knife-skewed,
Rolling and rolling there
Where God seems not to care;
Till the fierce Love they bear
Cramps them in death's extreme decrepitude.

Your voice sings not so soft, -
Though even as wind murmuring through raftered loft, -
Your dear voice is not dear,
Gentle, and evening clear,
As theirs whom none now hear,
Now earth has stopped their piteous mouths that coughed.

Heart, you were never hot,
Nor large, nor full like hearts made great with shot;
And though your hand be pale,
Paler are all which trail
Your cross through flame and hail:
Weep, you may weep, for you may touch them not.

ANONYMOUS POEMS

The north wind doth blow

The north wind doth blow,
And we shall have snow,
And what will poor Robin do then, poor thing?
He'll sit in a barn,
And keep himself warm
And hide his head under his wing, poor thing!

The north wind doth blow,
And we shall have snow,
And what will the swallow do then, poor thing?
Oh, do you not know
That he's off long ago,
To a country where he will find spring, poor thing!

The north wind doth blow,
And we shall have snow,
And what will the dormouse do then, poor thing?
Roll'd up like a ball,
In his nest snug and small,
He'll sleep till warm weather comes in, poor thing!

The north wind doth blow,
And we shall have snow,
And what will the honey-bee do then, poor thing?
In his hive he will stay
Till the cold is away,
And then he'll come out in the spring, poor thing!

The north wind doth blow,
And we shall have snow,
And what will the children do then, poor things?
When lessons are done
They must skip, jump and run,
Until they have made themselves warm, poor things!

Curley locks, Curley locks

Curley locks, curley locks wilt thou be mine?
Thou shalt not wash dishes nor yet feed the swine,
But sit on a cushion and sew a fine seam
And feed upon strawberries, sugar and cream.

The Streets of Laredo

As I walked out in the streets of Laredo,
As I walked out in Laredo one day,
I spied a young cowboy all wrapped in white linen,
All wrapped in white linen as cold as the clay.

'I see by your outfit that you are a cowboy'-
These words he did say as I boldly stepped by,
'Come sit down beside me and hear my sad story;
I'm shot in the breast and I know I must die.

'It was once in the saddle I used to go dashing,
Once in the saddle I used to go gay;
First to the ale-house and then to the jail-house,
Got shot in the breast and I'm dying today.

'Get six jolly cowboys to carry my coffin;
Get six pretty maidens to carry my pall;
Put bunches of roses all over my coffin,
Roses to deaden the clods as they fall.

'Oh, beat the drum slowly and play the fife lowly,
Play the dead march as you carry me along;
Take me to the green valley and lay the sod o'er me,
For I'm a young cowboy and I know I've done wrong.

'Go gather around you a crowd of young cowboys
And tell them the story of this, my sad fate;
Tell one and the other before they go further
To stop their wild roving before it's too late.

'Go fetch me a cup, a cup of cold water
To cool my parched lips,' the cowboy then said.
Before I returned, the spirit had left him
And gone to its Maker - the cowboy was dead.

We beat the drum slowly and played the fife lowly,
And bitterly wept as we carried him along;
For we all loved our comrade, so brave, young and handsome,
We all loved our comrade although he'd done wrong.

Poor but Honest

She was poor, but she was honest,
Victim of the squire's whim:
First he loved her, then he left her,
And she lost her honest name.

Then she ran away to London,
For to hide her grief and shame,
There she met another squire,
And she lost her name again.

See her riding in her carriage,
In the Park and all so gay:
All the nibs and nobby persons
Come to pass the time of day.

See the little old-world village
Where her aged parents live,
Drinking the champagne she sends them;
But they never can forgive.

In the rich man's arms she flutters,
Like a bird with broken wing:
First he loved her, then he left her,
And she hasn't got a ring.

See him in the splendid mansion,
Entertaining with the best,
While the girl that he has ruined,
Entertains a sordid guest.

See him in the House of Commons,
Making laws to put down crime.
While the victim of his passions
Trails her way through mud and slime.

Standing on the bridge at midnight.
She says: 'Farewell, blighted Love.'
There's a scream, a splash - Good Heavens!
What is she a-doing of?

Then they drag her from the river,
Water from her clothes they wrang.
For they thought that she was drownded;
But the corpse got up and sang:

'It's the same the whole world over:
It's the poor that gets the blame,
It's the rich that get the pleasure.
Isn't it a blooming shame?'

The Riddling Knight

There were three sisters fair and bright,
Jennifer, Gentle, and Rosemary,
And they three loved one valiant knight -
As the dow flies over the mulberry-tree.

The eldest sister let him in,
And barr'd the door with a silver pin.

The second sister made his bed,
And placed soft pillows under his head.

The youngest sister that same night
Was resolved for to wed wi' this valiant knight.

'And if you can answer questions three,
O then, fair maid, I'll marry wi' thee.

'O what is louder nor a horn,
Or what is sharper nor a thorn?

'Or what is heavier nor the lead,
Or what is better nor the bread?

'Or what is longer nor the way,
Or what is deeper nor the sea?'-

'O shame is louder nor a horn,
And hunger is sharper nor a thorn.

'O sin is heavier nor the lead,
The blessing's better nor the bread.

'O the wind is longer nor the way
And love is deeper nor the sea.'

'Your have answer'd aright my questions three,'
Jennifer, Gentle, and Rosemary;
'And now, fair maid, I'll marry wi' thee,'
As the dow flies over the mulberry-tree.

Charles Collins and Fred W Leigh

The Bridesmaid

Why am I dressed in these beautiful clothes?
What is the matter with me?
I've been the bridesmaid for twenty-two brides;
This time'll make twenty-three.
Twenty-two ladies I've helped off the shelf;
No doubt it seems a bit strange:
Being the bridesmaid is no good to me;
And I think could do with a change.

Why am I always the bridesmaid?
Never the blushing bride?
Ding-dong! wedding bells
Only ring for other gels;
But some fine day -
Oh, let it be soon! -
I shall wake up in the morning
On my own honeymoon.

Twenty two times have I gone to the church,
Followed the bride up the aisle,
Twenty two ladies have answered 'I will'
Meaning I won't all the while.
Twenty two couples I've seen go away,
Just him and her on their own,
Twenty two times I have wished it was me
And gone back home to Mother alone

CHORUS

I had a good chance a week or two back,
Took my young man home to tea.
Mother got playful and give him a pinch
Pinched my "financy" from me.
Being a widow she knew what to do,
No use for me to complain,
When they got married today, if you please
I was only the bridesmaid again.

CHORUS

Index of Poets

Laurence Alma Tadema (1836-1912)
Little Girls   120
Anonymous Poems
The north wind doth blow   132
Curley locks, curley locks   133
The Streets of Laredo   133
Poor but Honest   135
The Riddling Knight   137
Matthew Arnold (1822-1888)
Dover Beach   104
Philomela   106
Requiescat   107
Elizabeth Barratt Browning (1806-1861)
A Musical Instrument   86
Grief   88
A Man's Requirements   89
William Blake (1757-1827)
The Piper   60
O rose, thou art sick!   61
The Garden of Love   61
London   62
Tiger, Tiger burning bright   63
Rupert Brook (1887-1915)
The Soldier   127
Clouds   128
Robert Browning (1812-1889)
Pippa's Song   95
My Last Duchess   95
from The Pied Piper   97
Thomas Campion (1567?-1619)
Never Weather-Beaten Sail   35
Laura   36
Follow thy Fair Sun   37
John Clare (1793-1864)
Little Trotty Wagtail   78
The Vixen   79
Autumn   79

140

Sara Coleridge (1802-1850)
January Brings the Snow	84
The Mother	85
Trees	86

Charles Collins & Fred W Leigh
The Bridesmaid	138

William Congreve (1670-1729)
False though She Be	51
A Hue and Cry after Fair Amoret	51

Thomas Dekker (1570?-1641?)
A Cradle Song	38
Song	38
Oh, the Month of May	39

Emily Dickinson (1830-1886)
Because I could not stop for Death	108
The Waking Year	109
Like Rain it sounded till it curved	110

John Donne (1573-1631)
The Canonization	40
Song	42
A Hymn to God the Father	43

Michael Drayton (1563-1631)
Agincourt	28
The Crier	30
Since there's no help, come let us kiss and part	31

John Dryden (1631-1700)
Phyllis	48
To the Memory of Mr Oldham	49
Happy the Man	50

Thomas Ford (c.1580-1648)
There is a lady sweet and kind	44

Oliver Goldsmith (1730-1774)
Song	57
The Deserted Village *from* The Deserted Village	57
The Village Schoolmaster *from* The Deserted Village	58

John Keats (1795-1821)
To Autumn	80
On First Looking into Chapman's Homer	82
Song	83

Charles Kingsley (1819-1875)
Three Fishers went Sailing . . . 102
A Farewell . . . 103
The Sands of Dee . . . 103

John Lyly (1554?-1606)
Syrinx . . . 25
Cupid and Campaspe . . . 26
Daphne . . . 27

Alice Meynell (1847-1922)
The Rainy Summer . . . 121
In Manchester Square . . . 122
A Thrush Before Dawn . . . 122

John Milton (1608-1674)
Nymphs and Shepherds, Dance No More . . . 45
On His Blindness . . . 46
At A Solemn Music . . . 47

Edith Nesbit (1858-1924)
Child's Song in Spring . . . 124
In the Cabinet Drawer . . . 125
Baby's Birthday . . . 126

Wilfred Owen (1893-1918)
Futility . . . 129
The Send-Off . . . 130
Greater Love . . . 131

Alexander Pope (1688-1744)
On a Certain Lady at Court . . . 52
Know Thyself *from* An Essay on Man . . . 53
from the Rape of the Lock . . . 54

Sir Walter Raleigh (1552?-1618)
As You Came From the Holy Land . . . 18
A Description of Love . . . 20
The Passionate Man's Pilgrimage . . . 21

Christina Rossetti (1830-1894)
The Wind . . . 111
Song . . . 111
from Goblin Market . . . 112
Uphill . . . 118
Remember . . . 119

William Shakespeare (1564-1616)
Shall I compare thee to a summer's day?	32
When to the sessions of sweet silent thought	33
Fidele	34
When in disgrace with fortune and men's eyes	35

Percy Bysshe Shelley (1792-1822)
Ode to the West Wind	72
Love's Philosophy	76
To Jane : The Keen Stars Were Twinkling	77

Sir Philip Sidney (1554-1586)
Rural Poesy	23
The Nightingale	24
The Bargain	25

Edmund Spenser (1552?-1599)
Fresh Spring, the herald of love's mighty king	15
Behold, O Man *from* The Faerie Queene	16
There is a meadow *from* Prothalamion	17

Jane Taylor (1783-1824)
Twinkle, twinkle, little star	71

Samuel Taylor Coleridge (1772-1834)
Work without Hope	67
Hunting Song	68
Kubla Khan	68

Alfred, Lord Tennyson (1809-1892)
The Miller's Daughter	92
Tears, Idle Tears *from* The Princess	93
I come from haunts of coots and hern *from* The Brook	94

William Wordsworth (1770-1850)
She was a Phantom of Delight	64
from Ode: Intimations of Immortality	65
from Recollections of Early Childhood	
Louisa	66

Thomas Wyatt (1503?-1542)
Blame Not My Lute	11
Forget Not Yet	13
The Lover Compareth his State to a Ship in Perilous Storm Tossed on the Sea	14

Index of Poems

Agincourt *Michael Drayton*	28
As You Came From the Holy Land *Sir Walter Raleigh*	18
At a Solemn Music *John Milton*	47
Autumn *John Clare*	79
Baby's Birthday *Edith Nesbit*	126
The Bargain *Sir Philip Sidney*	25
Because I could not stop for Death *Emily Dickinson*	108
Behold, O Man *from* The Faerie Queene *Edmund Spenser*	16
Blame Not My Lute *Thomas Wyatt*	11
The Bridesmaid *Charles Collins and Fred W Leigh*	138
The Canonization *John Donne*	40
Child's Song in Spring *Edith Nesbit*	124
Clouds *Rupert Brooke*	128
A Cradle Song *Thomas Dekker*	38
The Crier *Michael Drayton*	30
Cupid and Campaspe *John Lyly*	26
Curley locks, curley locks *Anon*	133
Daphne *John Lyly*	27
A Description of Love *Sir Walter Raleigh*	20
The Deserted Village *from* The Deserted Village *Oliver Goldsmith*	57
Dover Beach *Matthew Arnold*	104
False though She Be *William Congreve*	51
A Farewell *Charles Kingsley*	103
Fidele *William Shakespeare*	34
Forget Not Yet *Thomas Wyatt*	13
Follow Thy Fair Sun *Thomas Campion*	37
Fresh Spring, the herald of love's mighty king *Edmund Spenser*	15
Futility *Wilfred Owen*	129
The Garden of Love *William Blake*	61
from Goblin Market *Christina Rossetti*	112
Greater Love *Wilfred Owen*	131
Grief *Elizabeth Barratt Browning*	88
Happy the Man *John Dryden*	50
A Hue and Cry after Fair Amoret *William Congreve*	51
Hunting Song *Samuel Taylor Coleridge*	68
A Hymn to God the Father *John Donne*	43
I come from haunts of coot and hern *from* The Brook *Alfred, Lord Tennyson*	94

In Manchester Square *Alice Meynell*	122
In the Cabinet Drawer *Edith Nesbit*	125
January brings the snow *Sara Coleridge*	84
Know Thyself *from* An Essay on Man *Alexander Pope*	53
Kubla Khan *Samuel Taylor Coleridge*	68
Laura *Thomas Campion*	36
Like Rain it sounded till it curved *Emily Dickinson*	110
Little Trotty Wagtail *John Clare*	78
Little Girls *Laurence Alma Tadema*	120
London *William Blake*	62
Louisa *William Wordsworth*	66
The Lover Compareth his State to a Ship in Perilous Storm Tossed on the Sea *Thomas Wyatt*	14
Love's Philosophy *Percy Bysshe Shelley*	76
A Man's Requirements *Elizabeth Barratt Browning*	89
The Miller's Daughter *Alfred, Lord Tennyson*	92
The Mother *Sara Coleridge*	85
A Musical Instrument *Elizabeth Barratt Browning*	86
My Last Duchess *Robert Browning*	95
Never Weather-Beaten Sail *Thomas Campion*	35
The Nightingale *Sir Philip Sidney*	24
The north wind doth blow *Anon*	132
Nymphs and Shepherds, Dance No More *John Milton*	45
from Ode: Intimations of Immortality from Recollections of Early Childhood *William Wordsworth*	65
Ode to the West Wind *Percy Bysshe Shelley*	72
Oh, the Month of May *Thomas Dekker*	39
On a Certain Lady at Court *Alexander Pope*	52
On First Looking into Chapman's Homer *John Keats*	82
On his Blindness *John Milton*	46
The Passionate Man's Pilgrimage *Sir Walter Raleigh*	21
Philomela *Matthew Arnold*	106
Phyllis *John Dryden*	48
from The Pied Piper *Robert Browning*	97
The Piper *William Blake*	60
Pippa's Song *Robert Browning*	95
Poor but Honest *Anon*	135
The Rainy Summer *Alice Meynell*	121
from The Rape of the Lock *Alexander Pope*	54
Requiescat *Matthew Arnold*	107
Remember *Christina Rossetti*	119

The Riddling Knight *Anon*	137
O rose, thou art sick! *William Blake*	61
Rural Poesy *Sir Philip Sidney*	23
The Sands of Dee *Charles Kingsley*	103
The Send-Off *Wilfred Owen*	130
Shall I compare thee to a summer's day? *William Shakespeare*	32
She was a Phantom of Delight *William Wordsworth*	64
Since there's no help, come let us kiss and part *Michael Drayton*	31
The Soldier *Rupert Brooke*	127
Song *Thomas Dekker*	38
Song *John Donne*	42
Song *Oliver Goldsmith*	57
Song *John Keats*	83
Song *Christina Rossetti*	111
The Streets of Laredo *Anon*	133
Syrinx *John Lyly*	25
Tears, Idle Tears *from* The Princess *Alfred, Lord Tennyson*	93
There is a lady sweet and kind *Thomas Ford*	44
There is a meadow *from* Prothalamion *Edmund Spenser*	17
Three Fishers went Sailing *Charles Kingsley*	102
A Thrush Before Dawn *Alice Meynell*	122
Tiger, Tiger burning bright *William Blake*	63
To Autumn *John Keats*	80
To Jane: The Keen Stars Were Twinkling *Percy Bysshe Shelley*	77
To the Memory of Mr Oldham *John Dryden*	49
Trees *Sara Coleridge*	86
Twinkle, twinkle, little star *Jane Taylor*	71
Uphill *Christina Rossetti*	118
The Village Schoolmaster *from* The Deserted Village *Oliver Goldsmith*	58
The Vixen *John Clare*	79
The Waking Year *Emily Dickinson*	109
When in disgrace with fortune and men's eyes *William Shakespeare*	35
When to the sessions of sweet silent thought *William Shakespeare*	33
The Wind *Christina Rossetti*	111
Work without Hope *Samuel Taylor Coleridge*	67